Adult Coloring Book Of Nasty Really Bad Swear Words

Woodrow Guy

This is a Bleed Through Page If You Are Using a Coloring Marker or Pen!

Find Other Great Titles By Us. Search on Your Favorite Book Retailer

Just search for the author name of Woodrow Guy .

He also Publishes Lite Erotica on Amazon Kindle

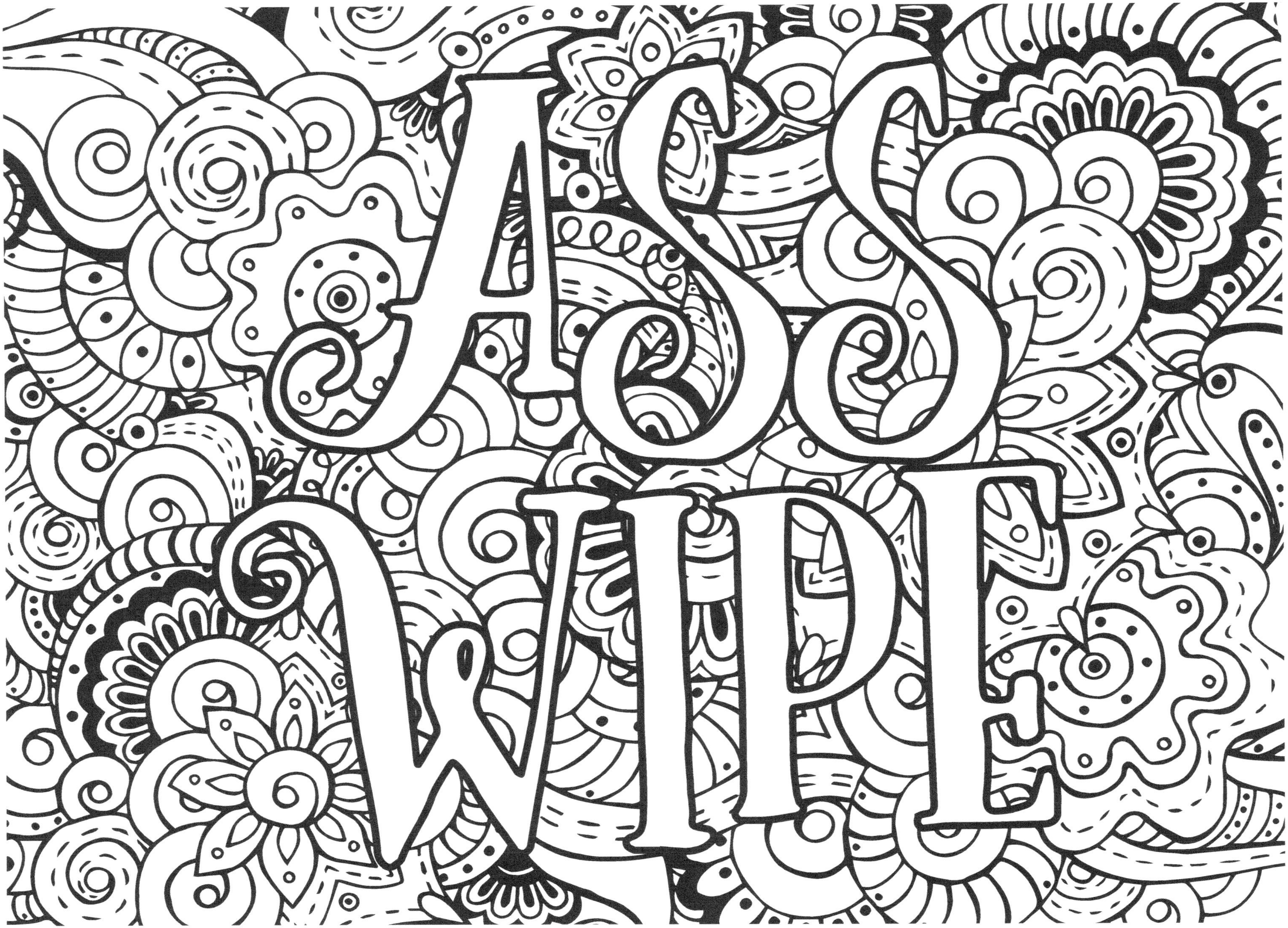
ASS
WIPE

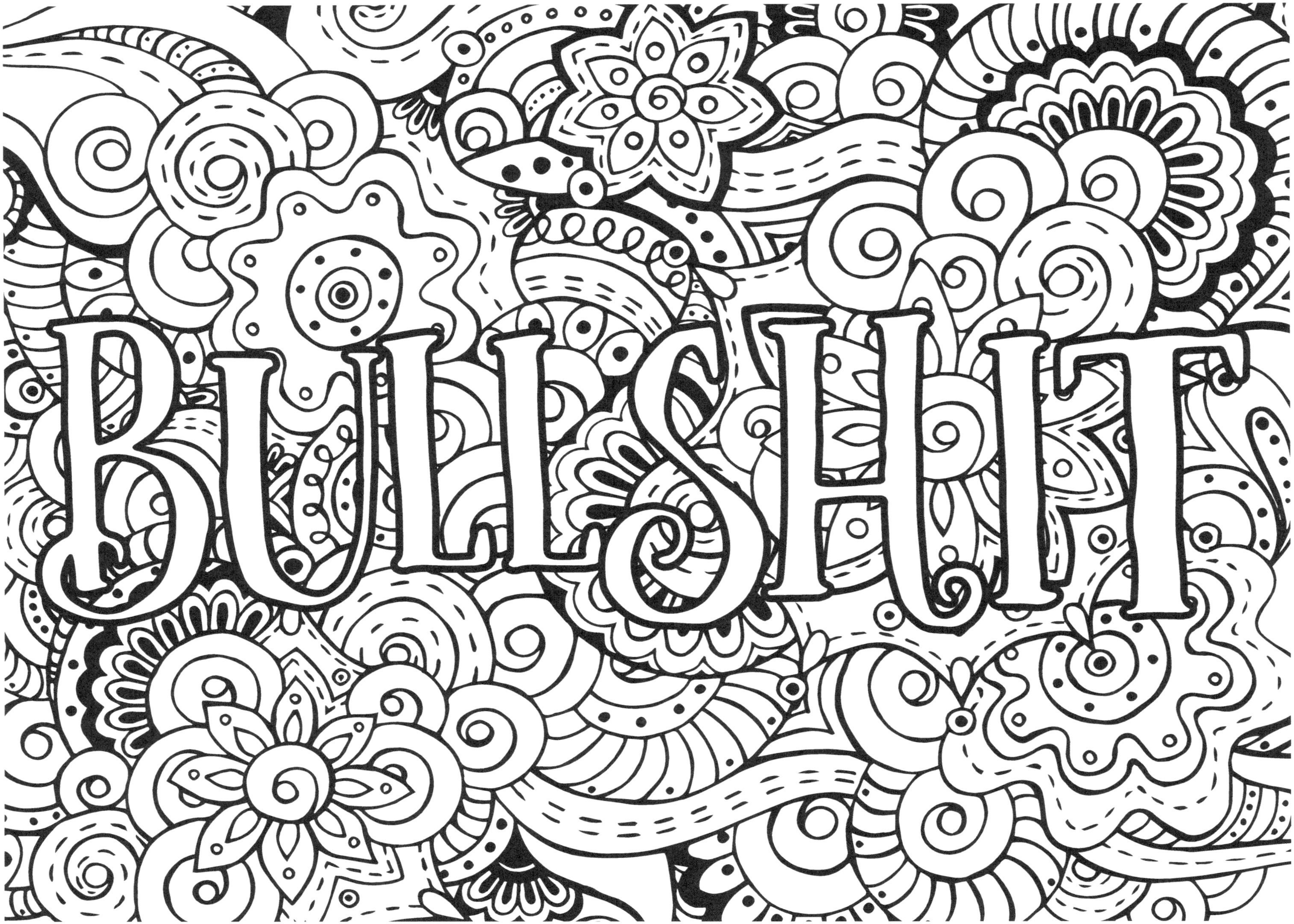
BULLSHIT

This is a Bleed Through Page If You Are Using a Coloring Marker or Pen!
Find Other Great Titles By Us. Search on Your Favorite Book Retailer
Just search for the author name of Woodrow Guy .
He also Publishes Lite Erotica on Amazon Kindle

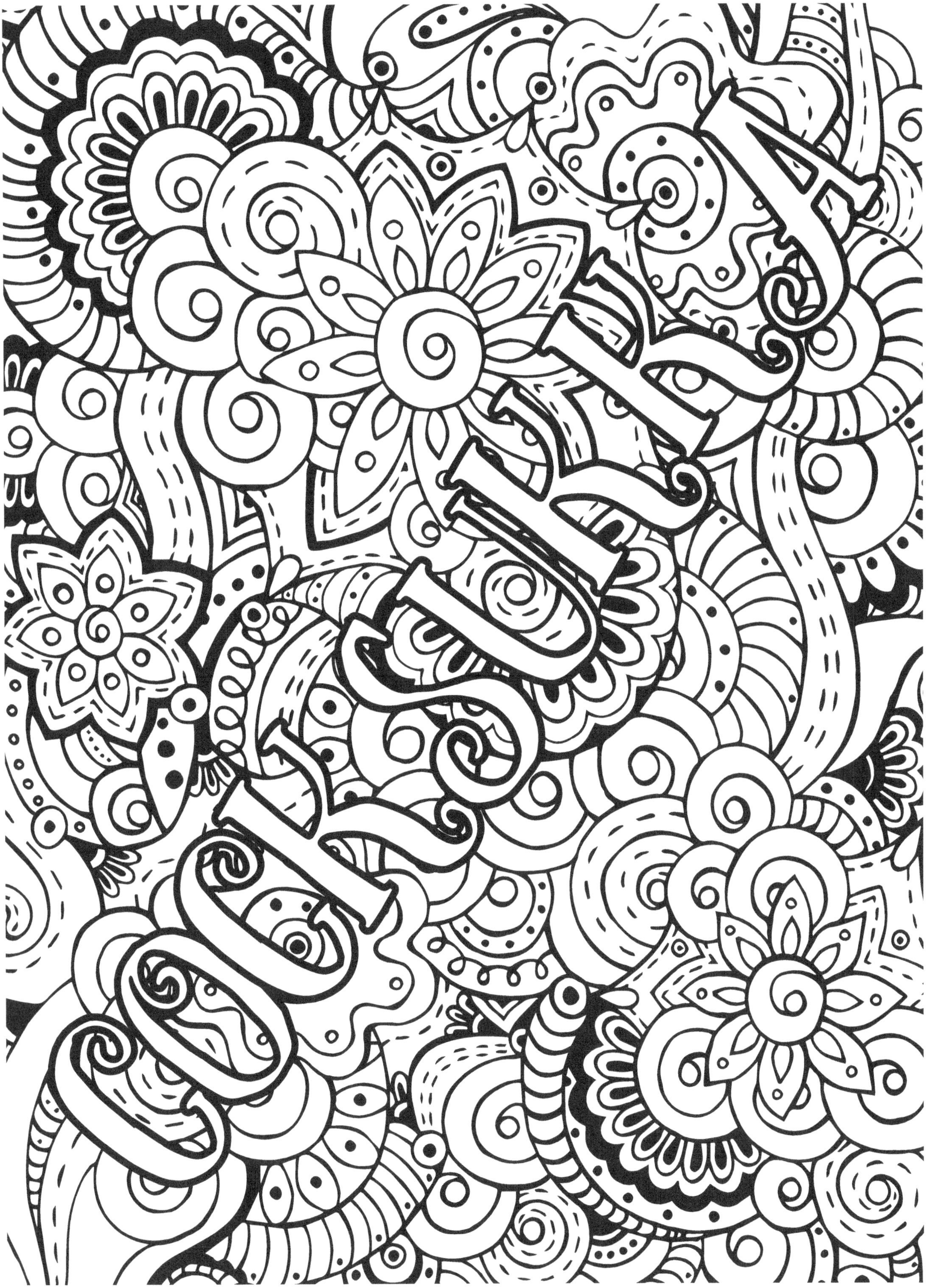

This is a Bleed Through Page If You Are Using a Coloring Marker or Pen!
Find Other Great Titles By Us. Search on Your Favorite Book Retailer
Just search for the author name of Woodrow Guy .
He also Publishes Lite Erotica on Amazon Kindle

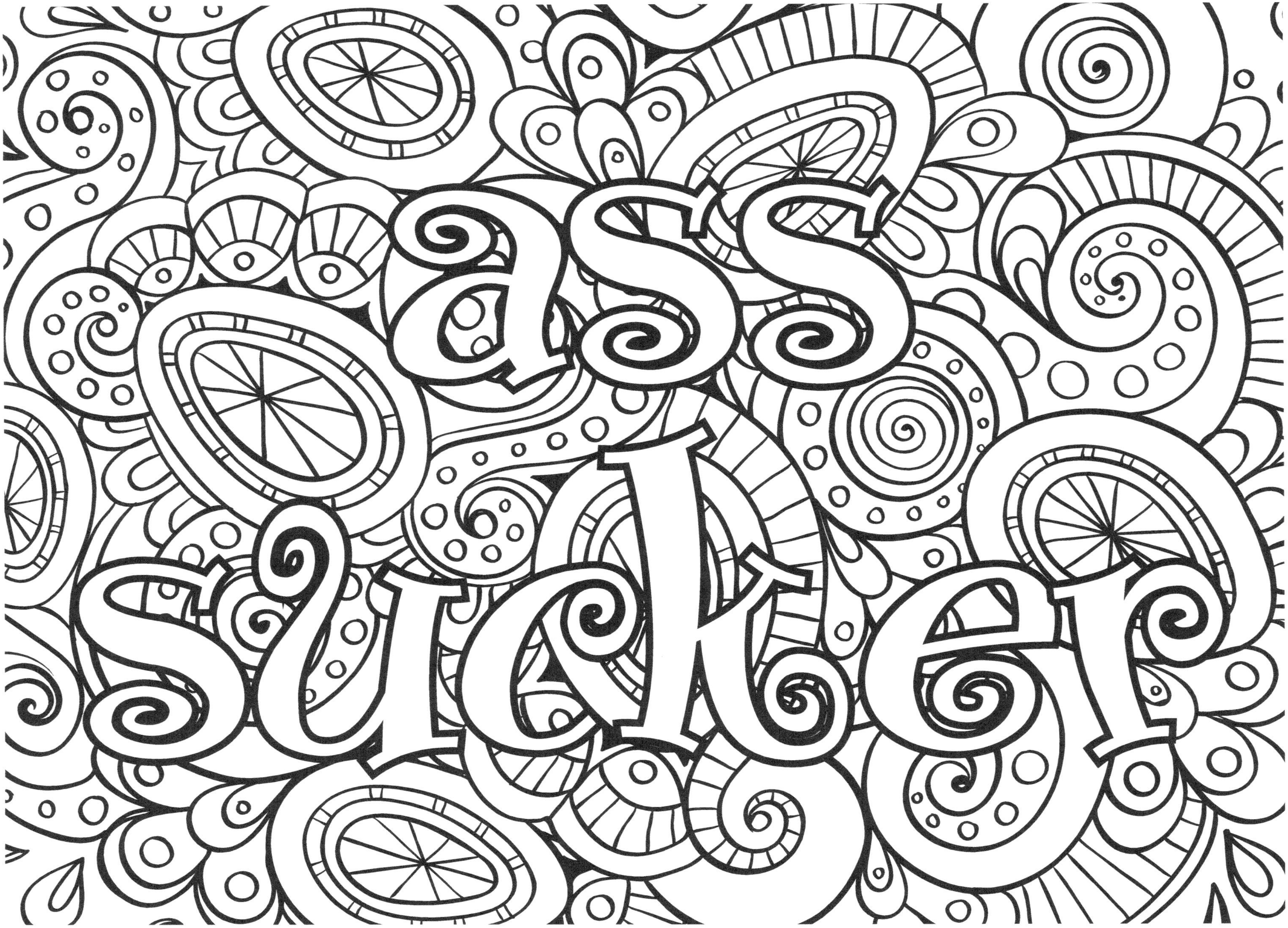
ass
sucker

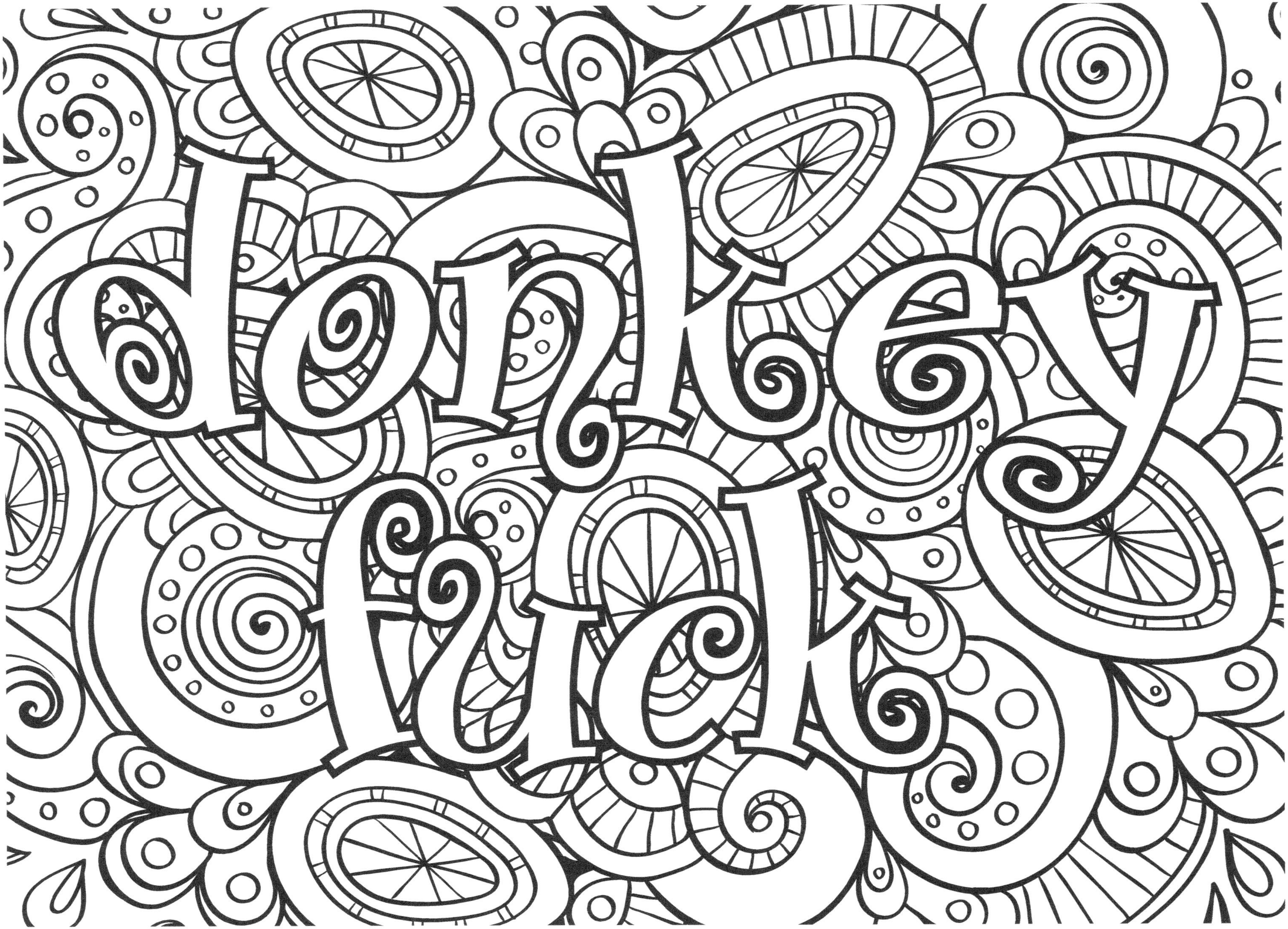
donkey
fuck

This is a Bleed Through Page If You Are Using a Coloring Marker or Pen!

Find Other Great Titles By Us. Search on Your Favorite Book Retailer

Just search for the author name of Woodrow Guy .

He also Publishes Lite Erotica on Amazon Kindle

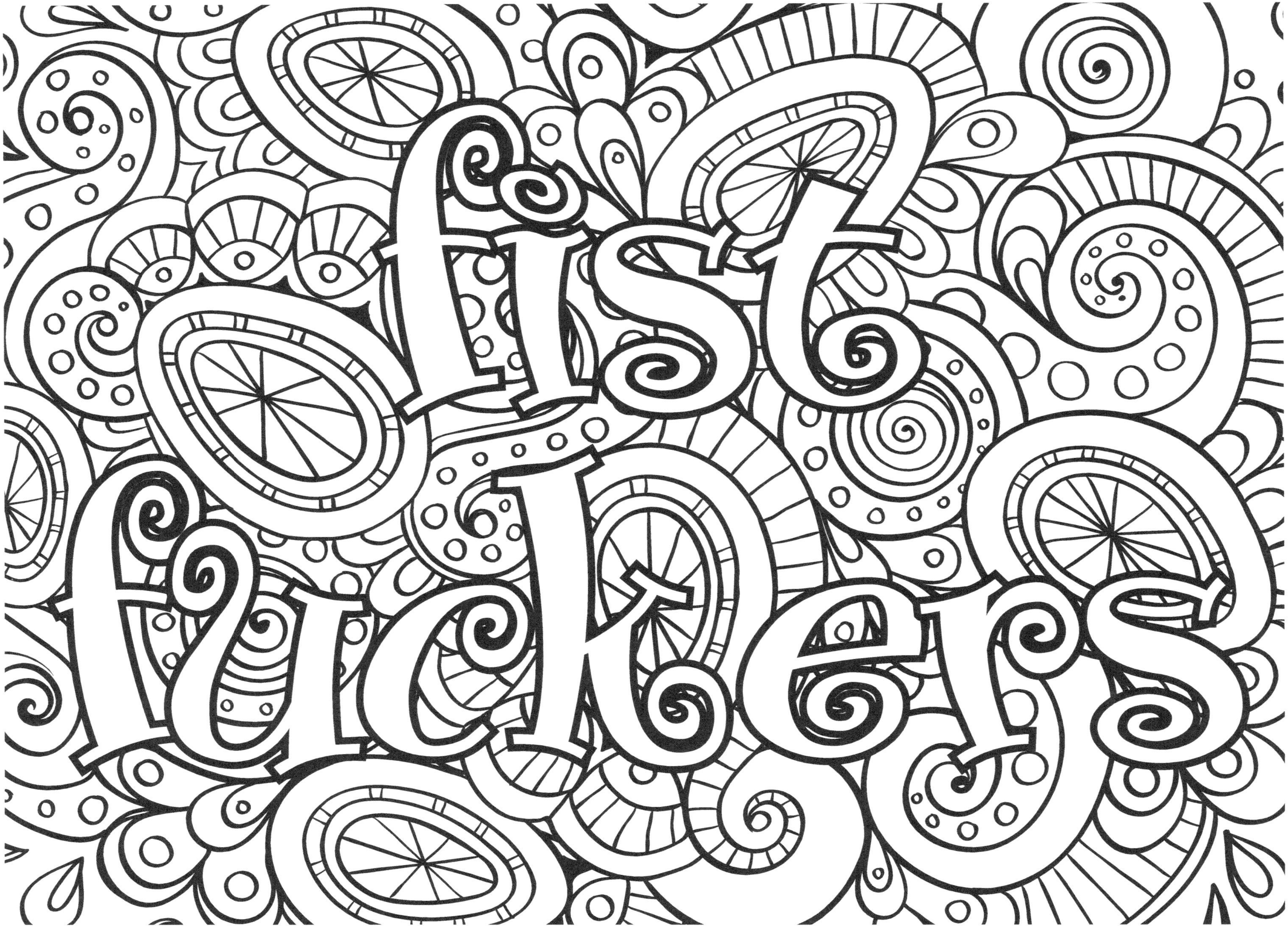
fist
fuckers

This is a Bleed Through Page If You Are Using a Coloring Marker or Pen!

Find Other Great Titles By Us. Search on Your Favorite Book Retailer

Just search for the author name of Woodrow Guy .

He also Publishes Lite Erotica on Amazon Kindle

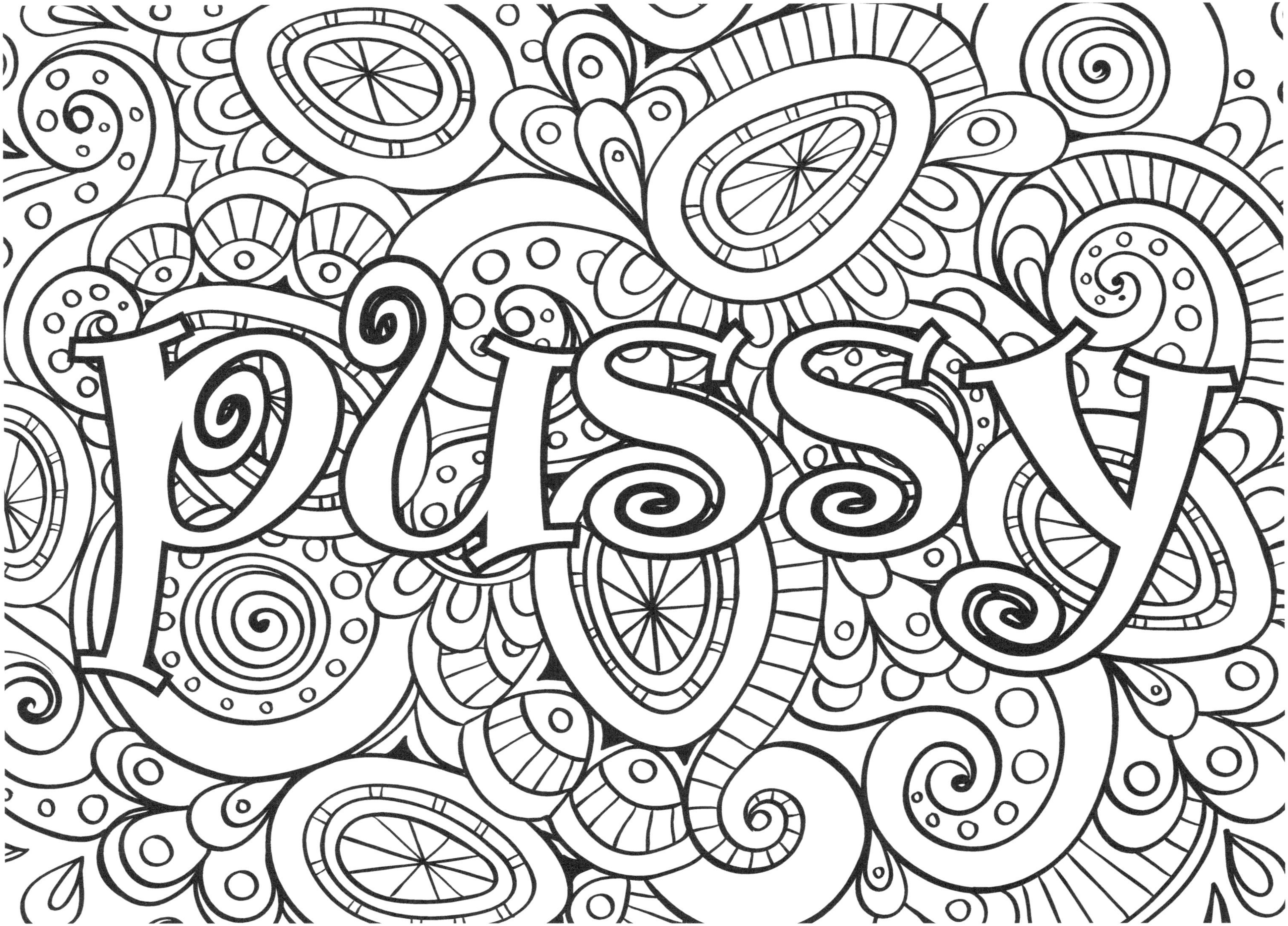
pussy

This is a Bleed Through Page If You Are Using a Coloring Marker or Pen!
Find Other Great Titles By Us. Search on Your Favorite Book Retailer
Just search for the author name of Woodrow Guy .
He also Publishes Lite Erotica on Amazon Kindle

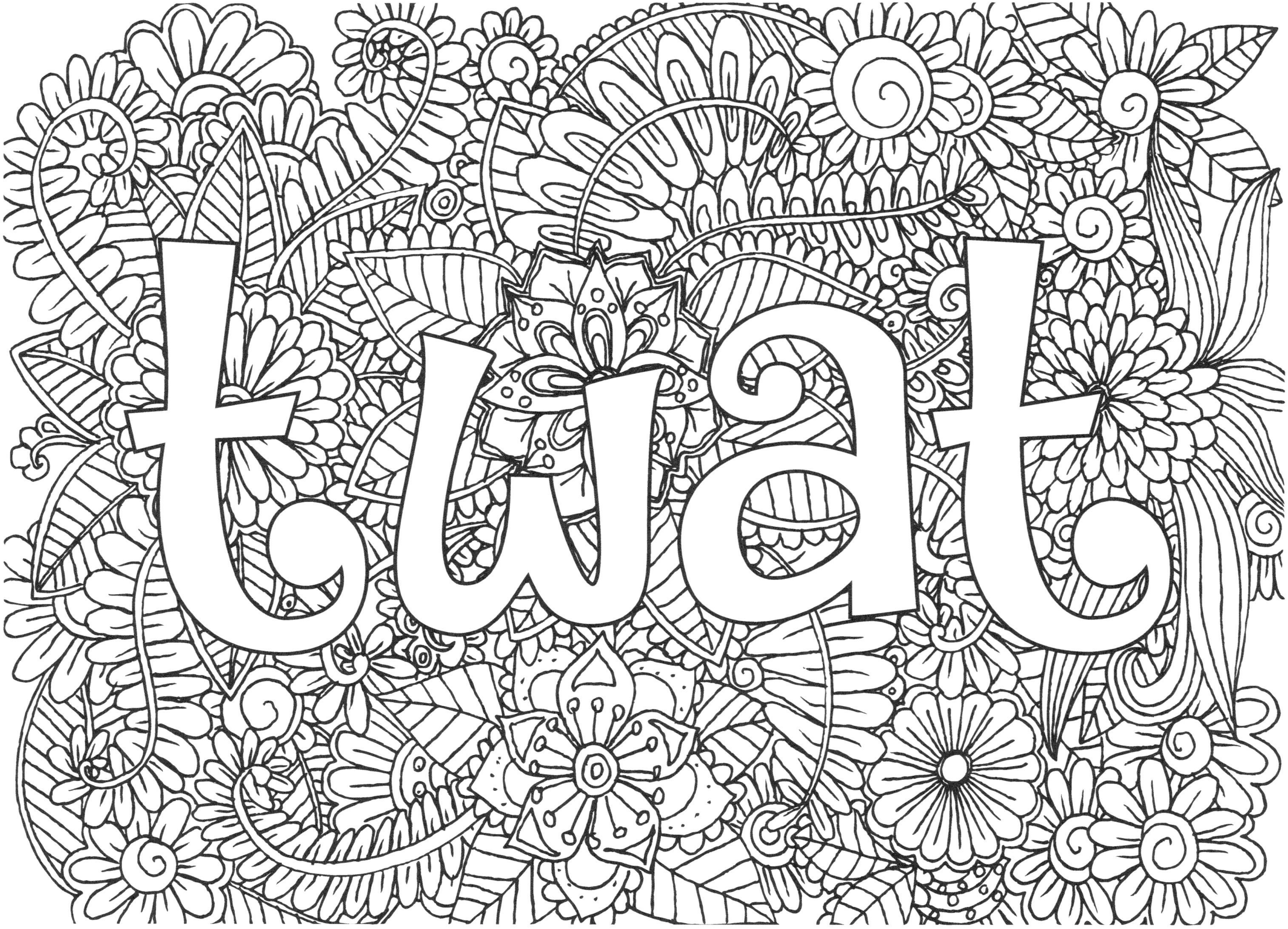
twat

This is a Bleed Through Page If You Are Using a Coloring Marker or Pen!
Find Other Great Titles By Us. Search on Your Favorite Book Retailer
Just search for the author name of Woodrow Guy .
He also Publishes Lite Erotica on Amazon Kindle

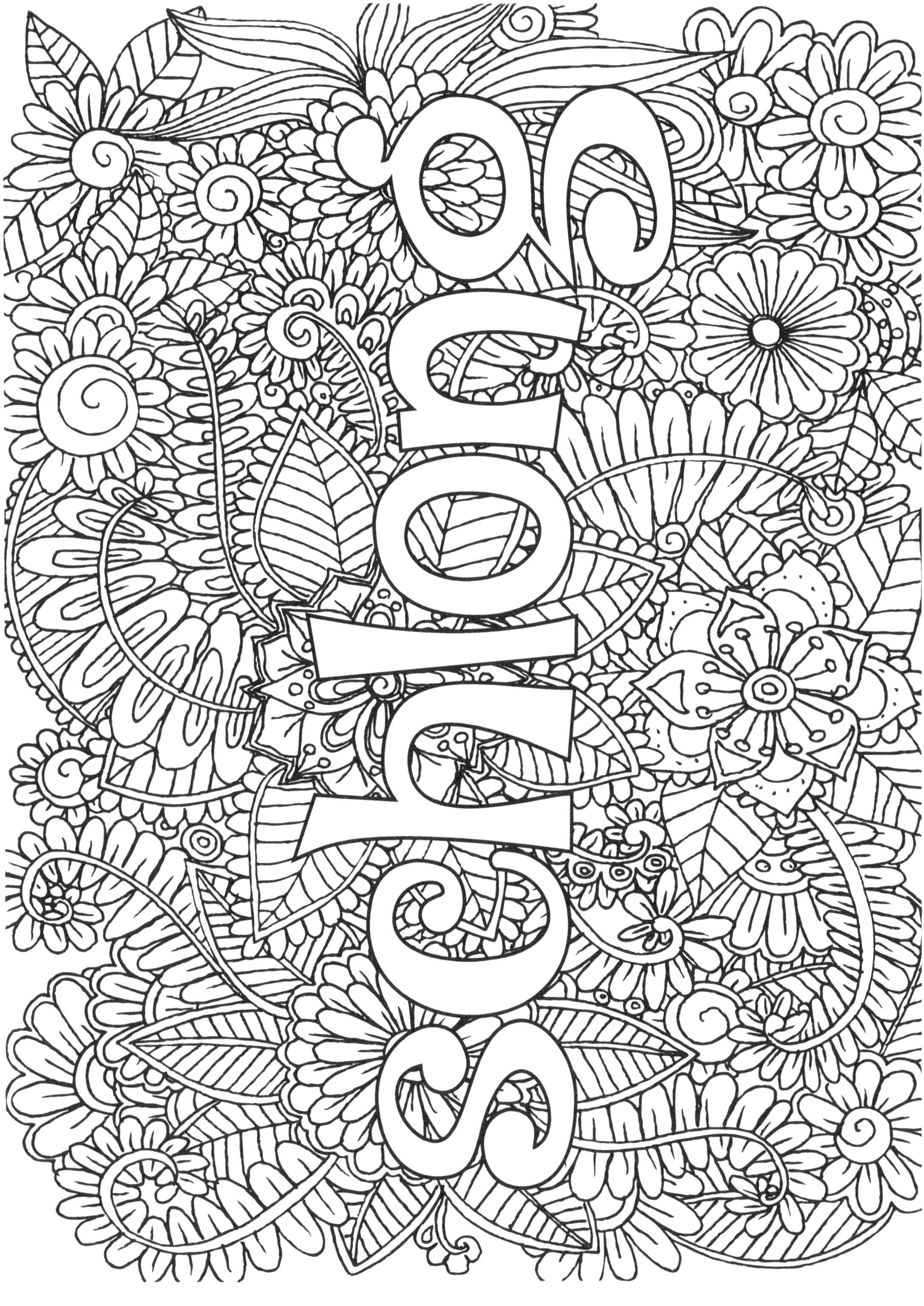
schlong

This is a Bleed Through Page If You Are Using a Coloring Marker or Pen!
Find Other Great Titles By Us. Search on Your Favorite Book Retailer
Just search for the author name of Woodrow Guy .
He also Publishes Lite Erotica on Amazon Kindle

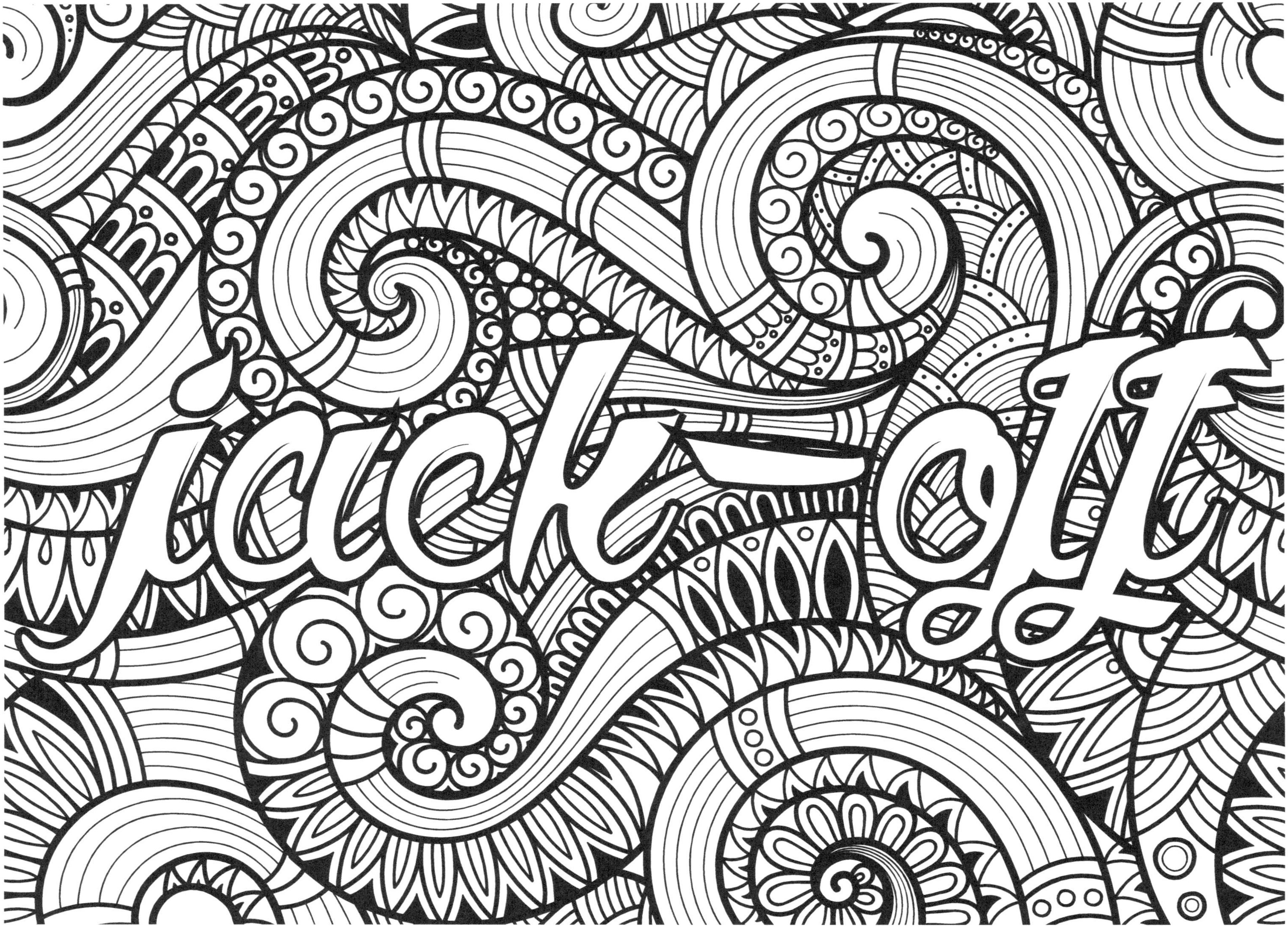
fuck-off

This is a Bleed Through Page If You Are Using a Coloring Marker or Pen!
Find Other Great Titles By Us. Search on Your Favorite Book Retailer
Just search for the author name of Woodrow Guy .
He also Publishes Lite Erotica on Amazon Kindle

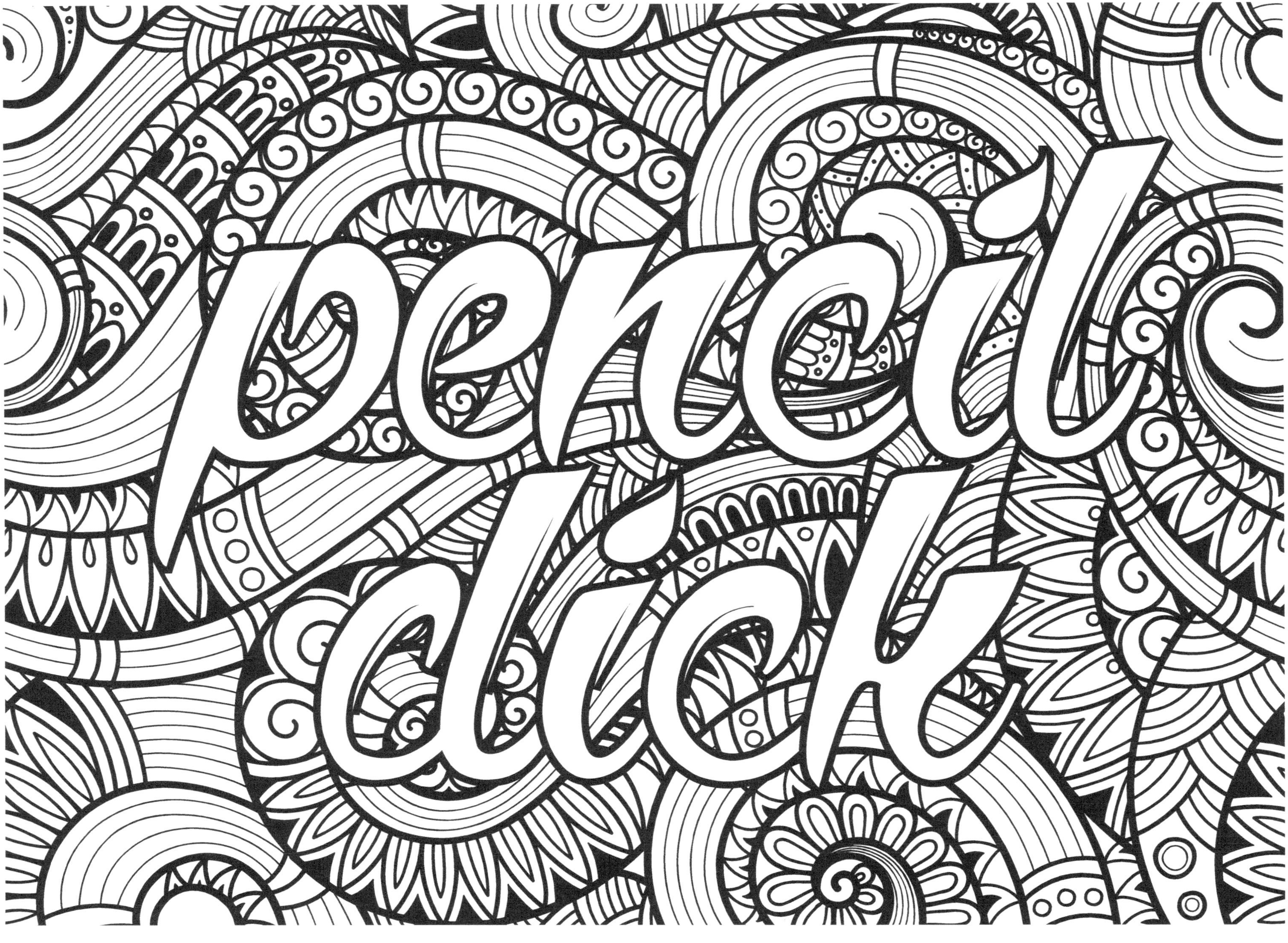
pencil
dick

This is a Bleed Through Page If You Are Using a Coloring Marker or Pen!
Find Other Great Titles By Us. Search on Your Favorite Book Retailer
Just search for the author name of Woodrow Guy .
He also Publishes Lite Erotica on Amazon Kindle

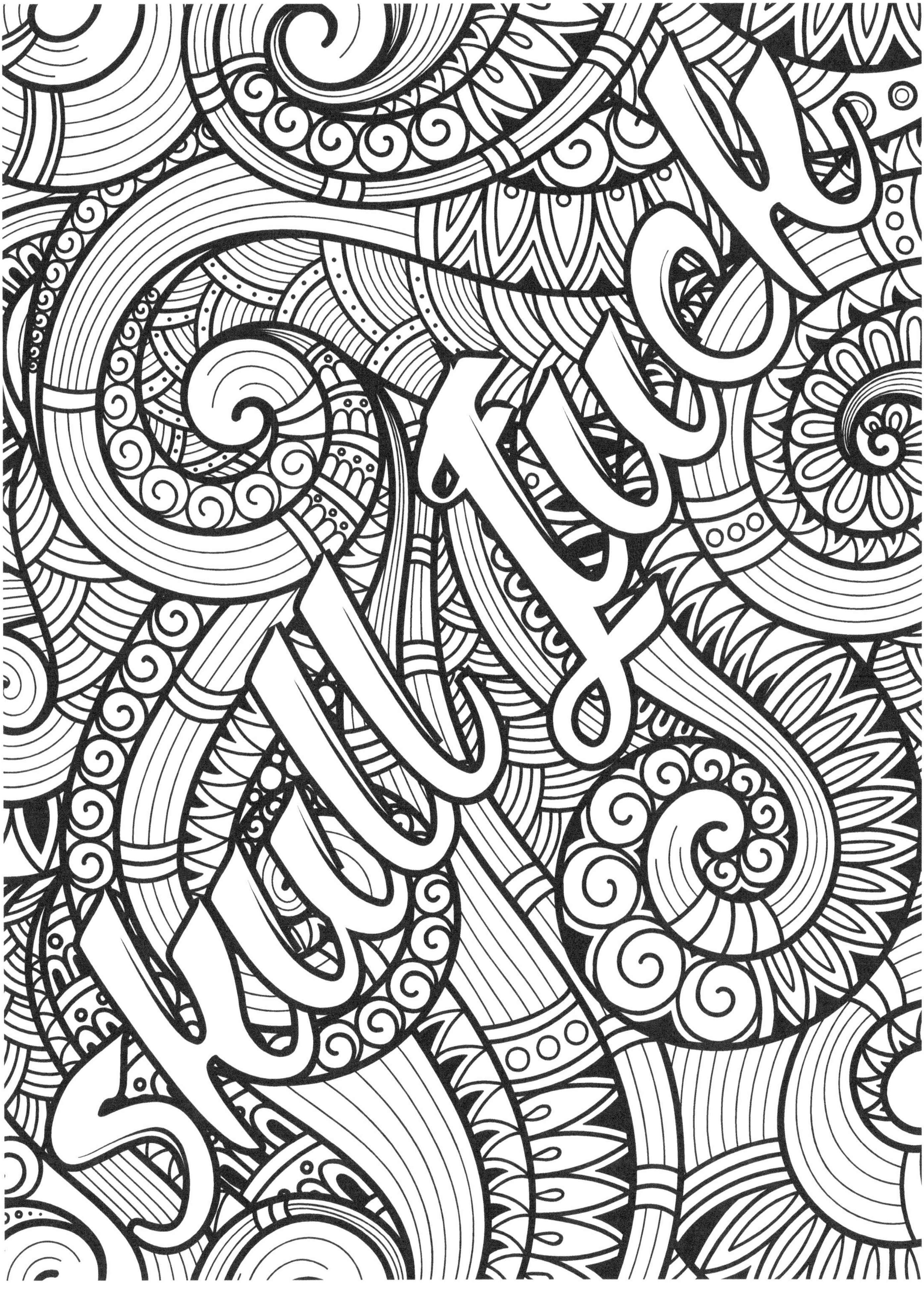
Skullfuck

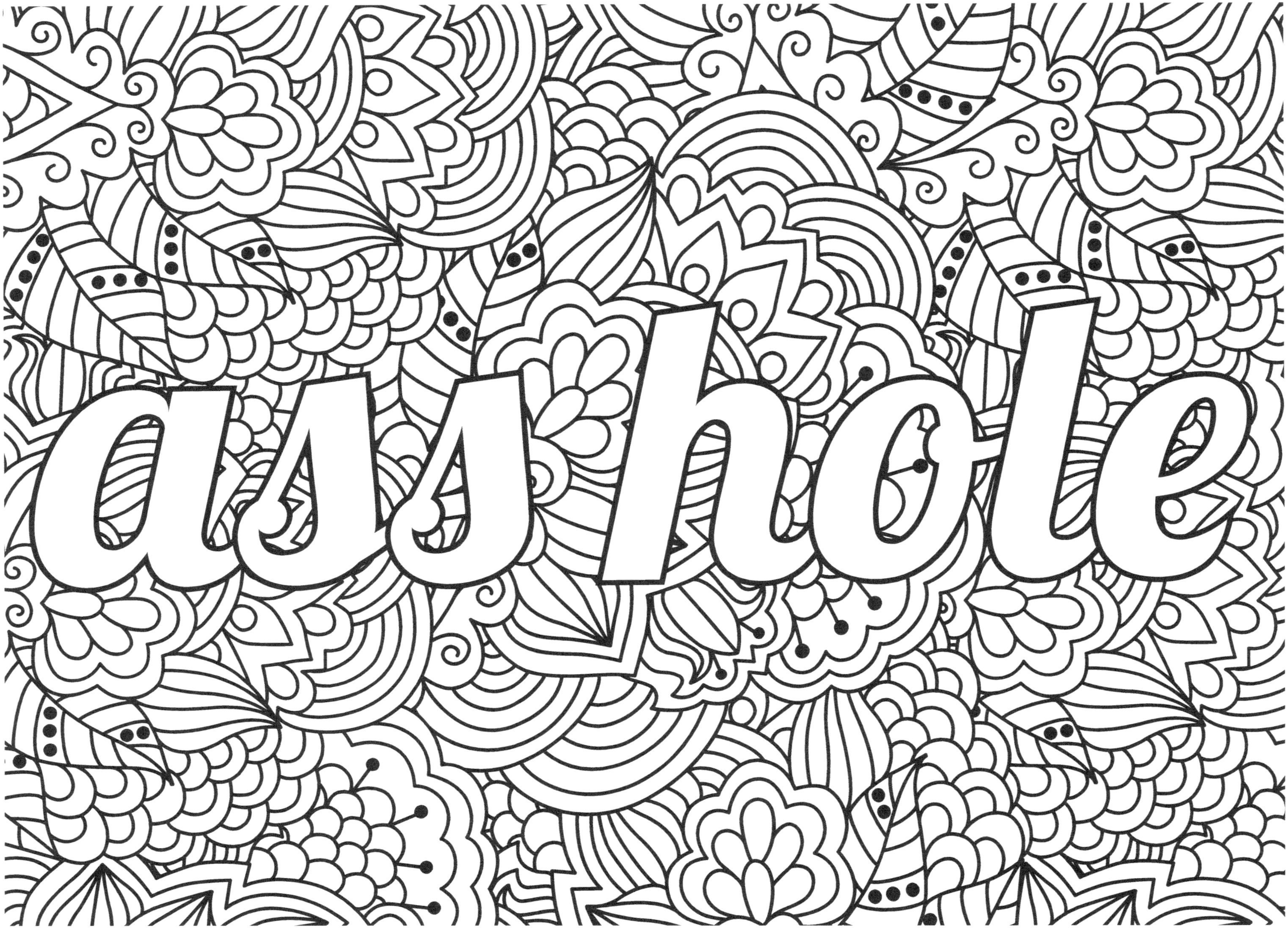
asshole

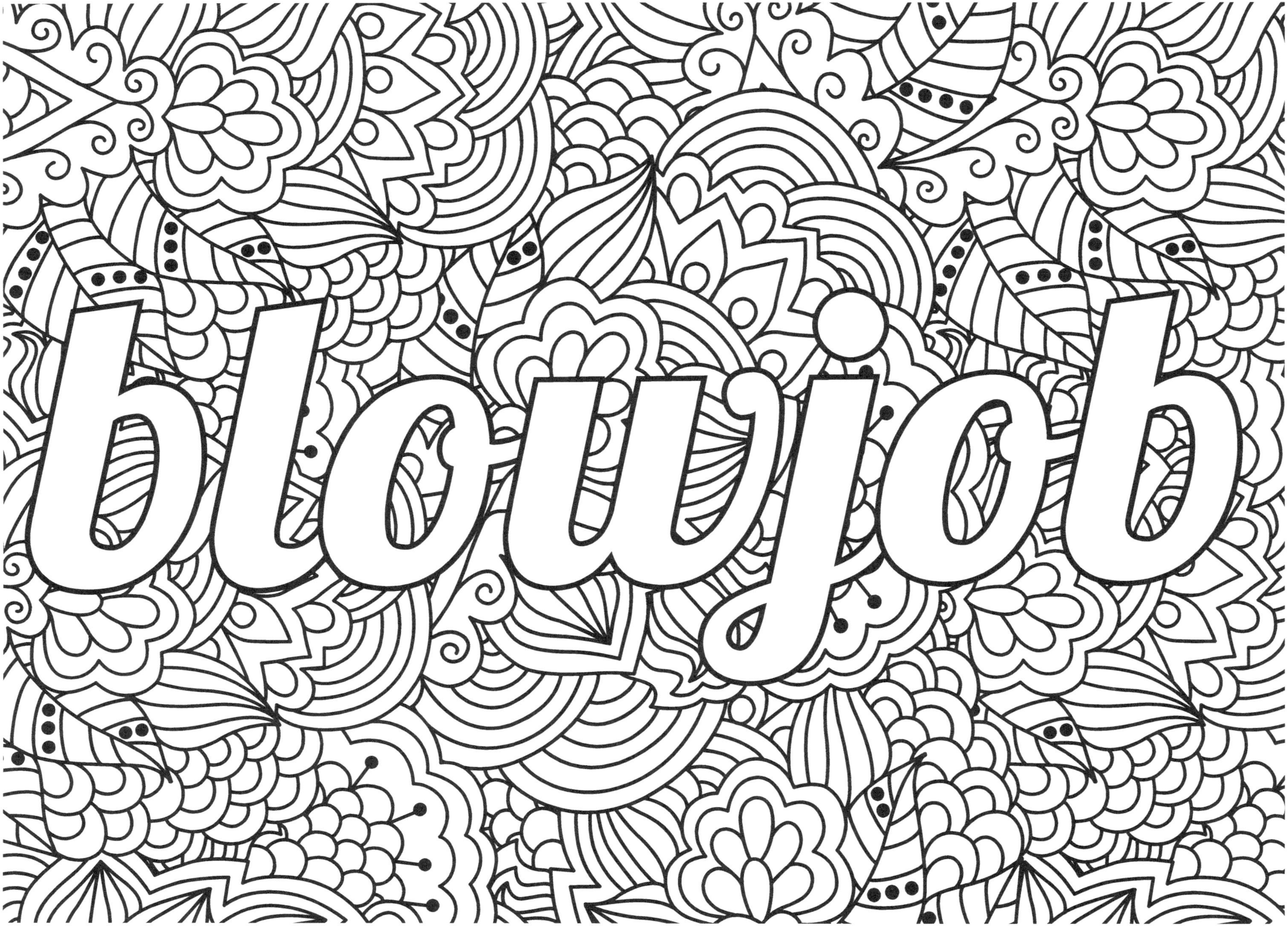
blowjob

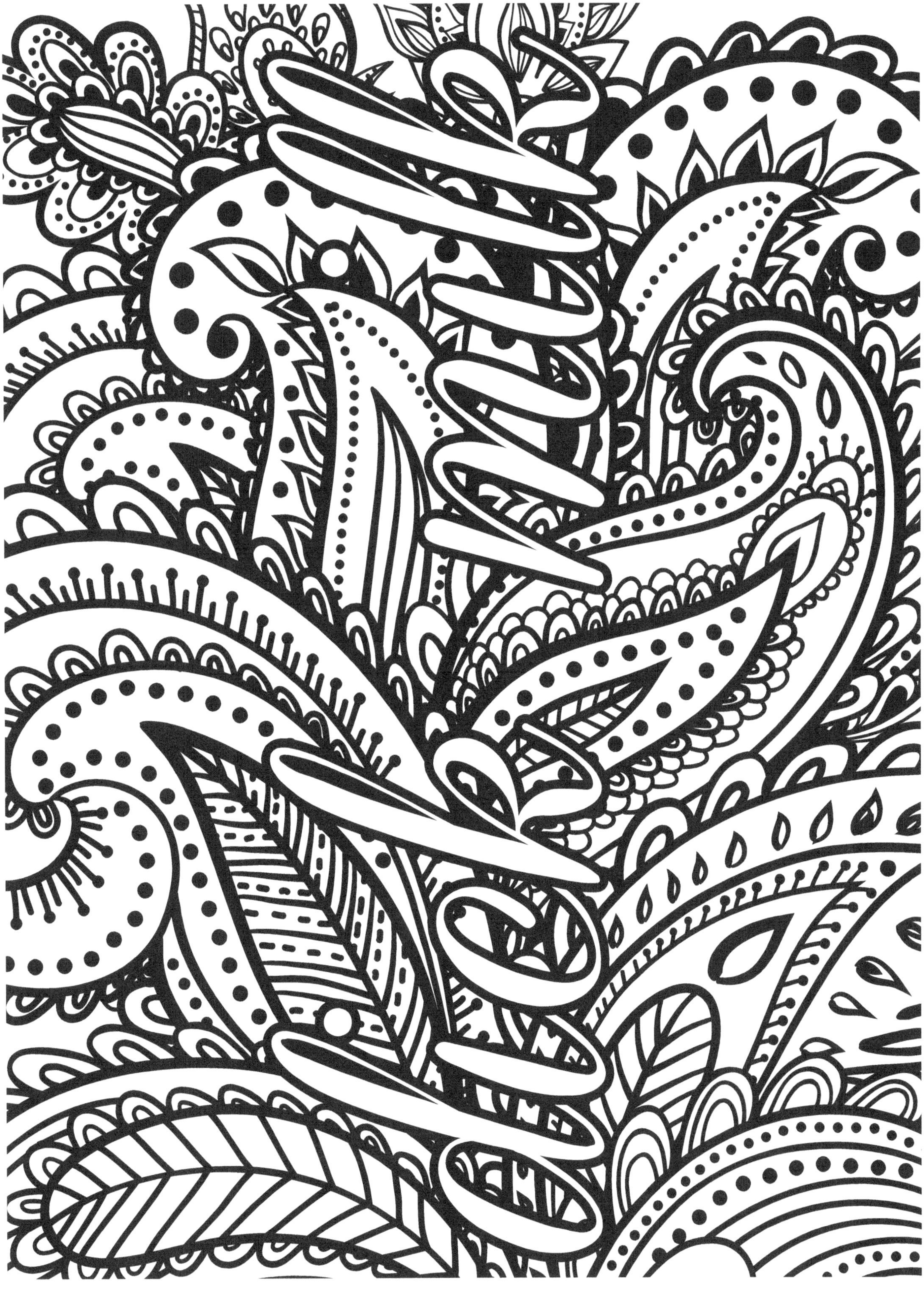
dick milk

This is a Bleed Through Page If You Are Using a Coloring Marker or Pen!
Find Other Great Titles By Us. Search on Your Favorite Book Retailer
Just search for the author name of Woodrow Guy .
He also Publishes Lite Erotica on Amazon Kindle

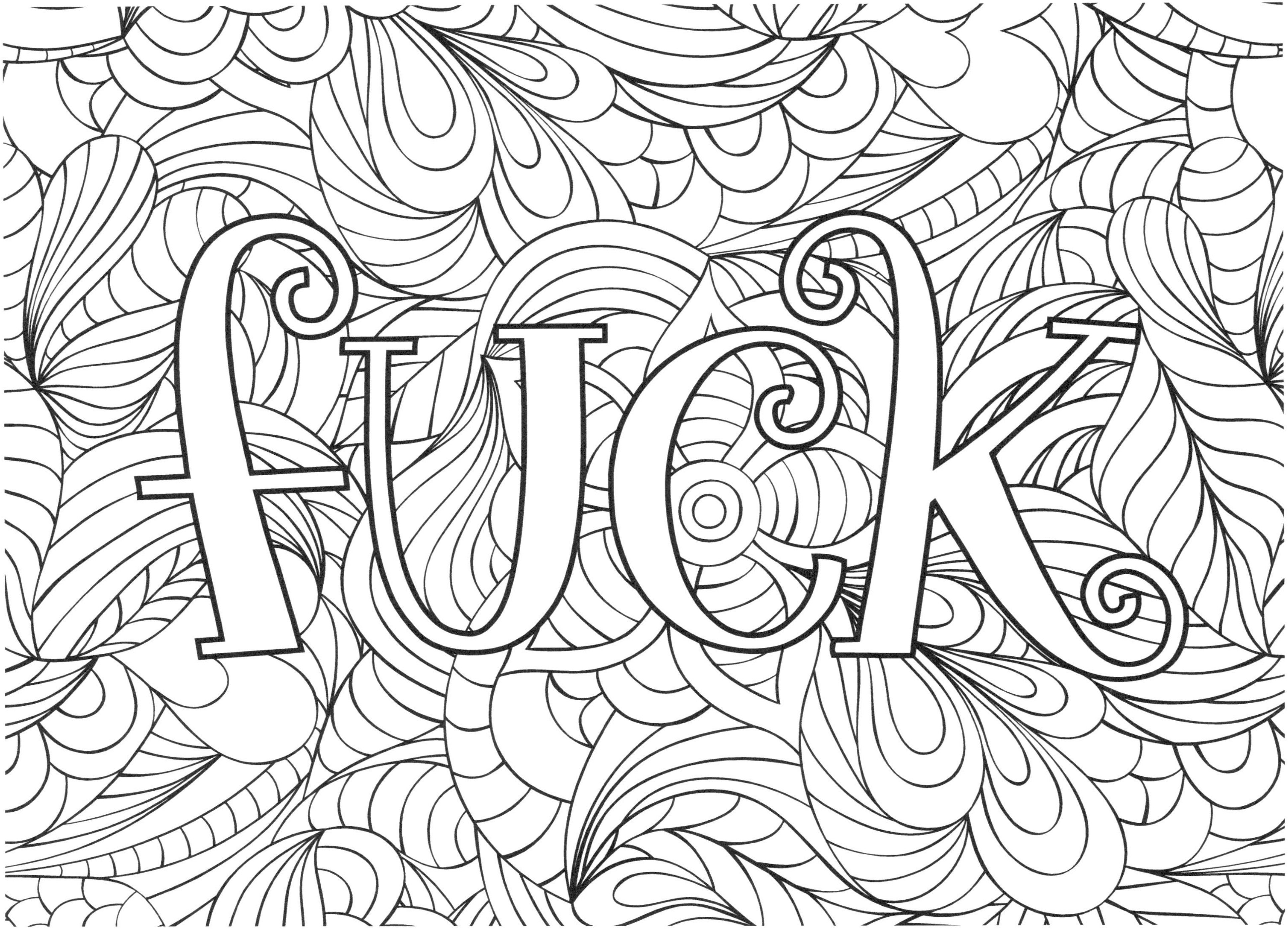
fuck

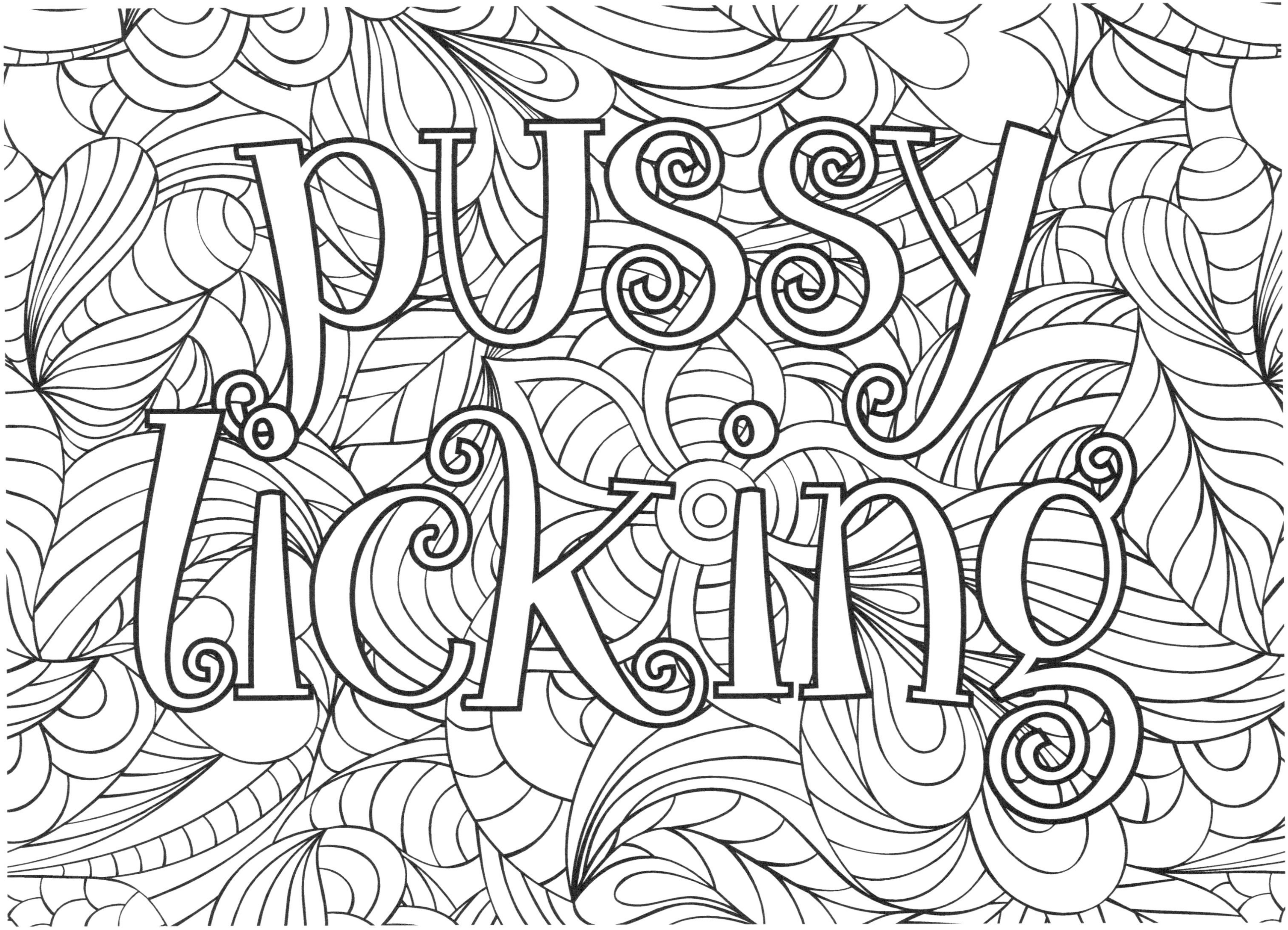
pussy
licking

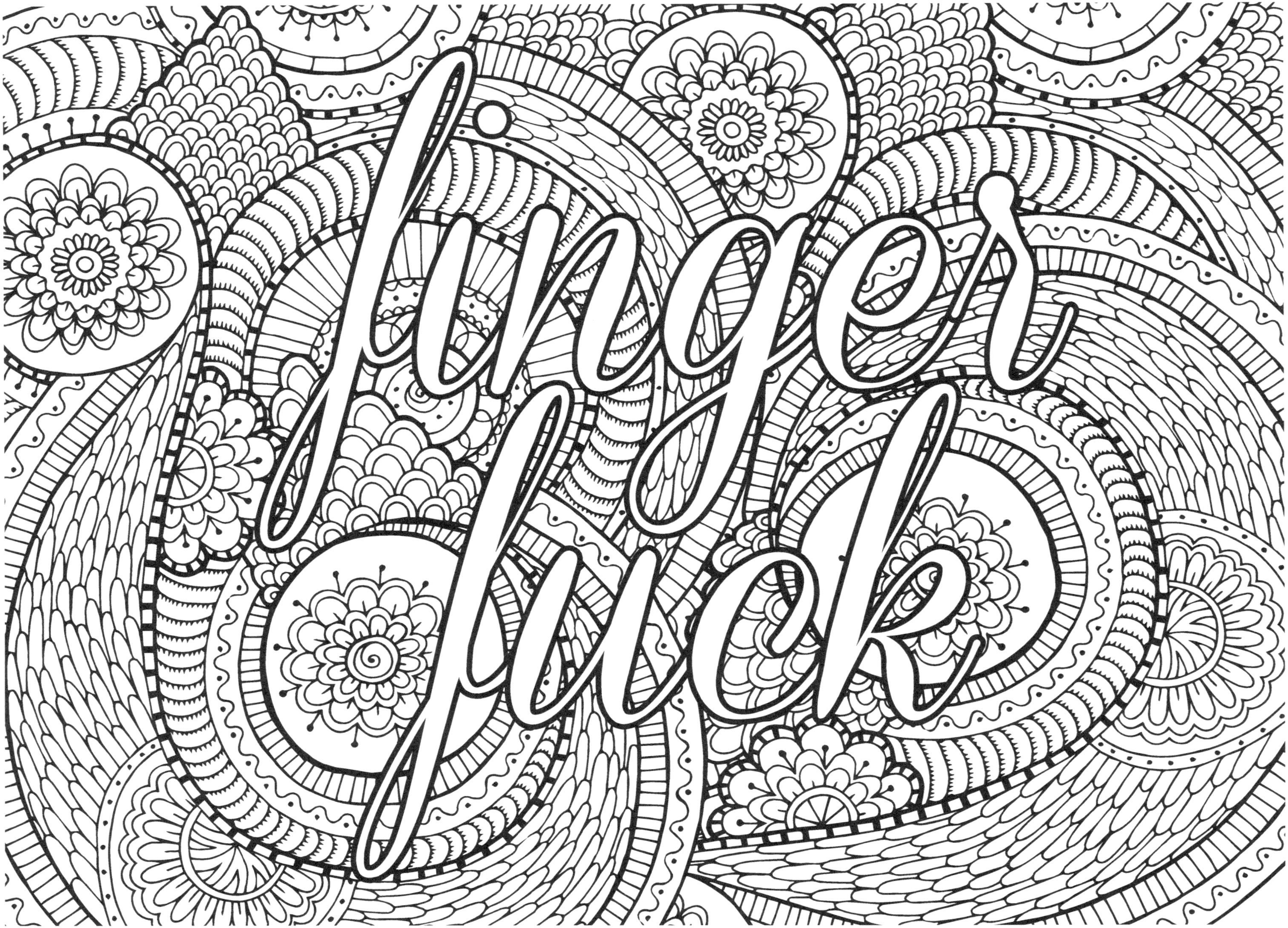
finger
fuck

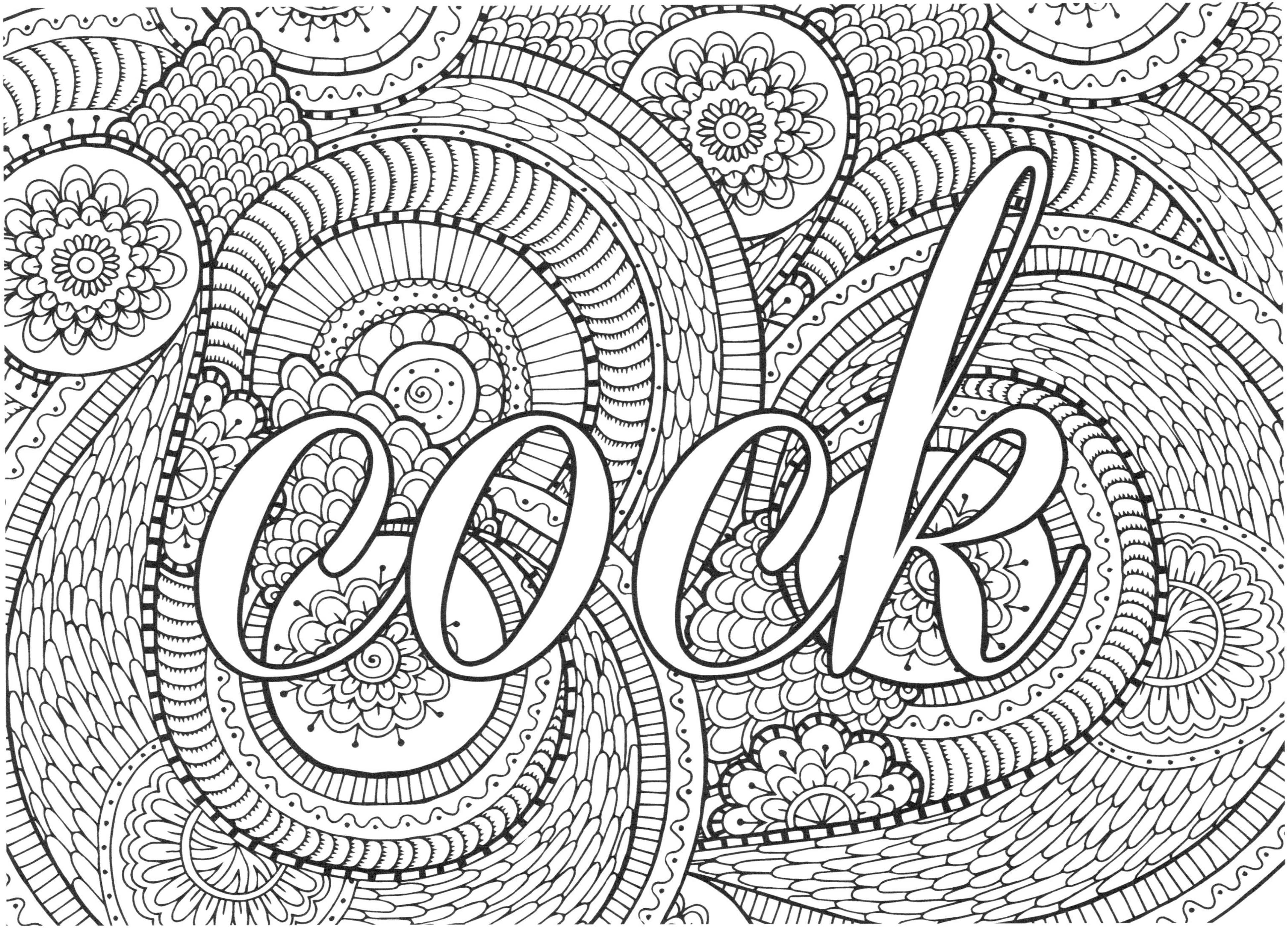
cock

This is a Bleed Through Page If You Are Using a Coloring Marker or Pen!
Find Other Great Titles By Us. Search on Your Favorite Book Retailer
Just search for the author name of Woodrow Guy .
He also Publishes Lite Erotica on Amazon Kindle

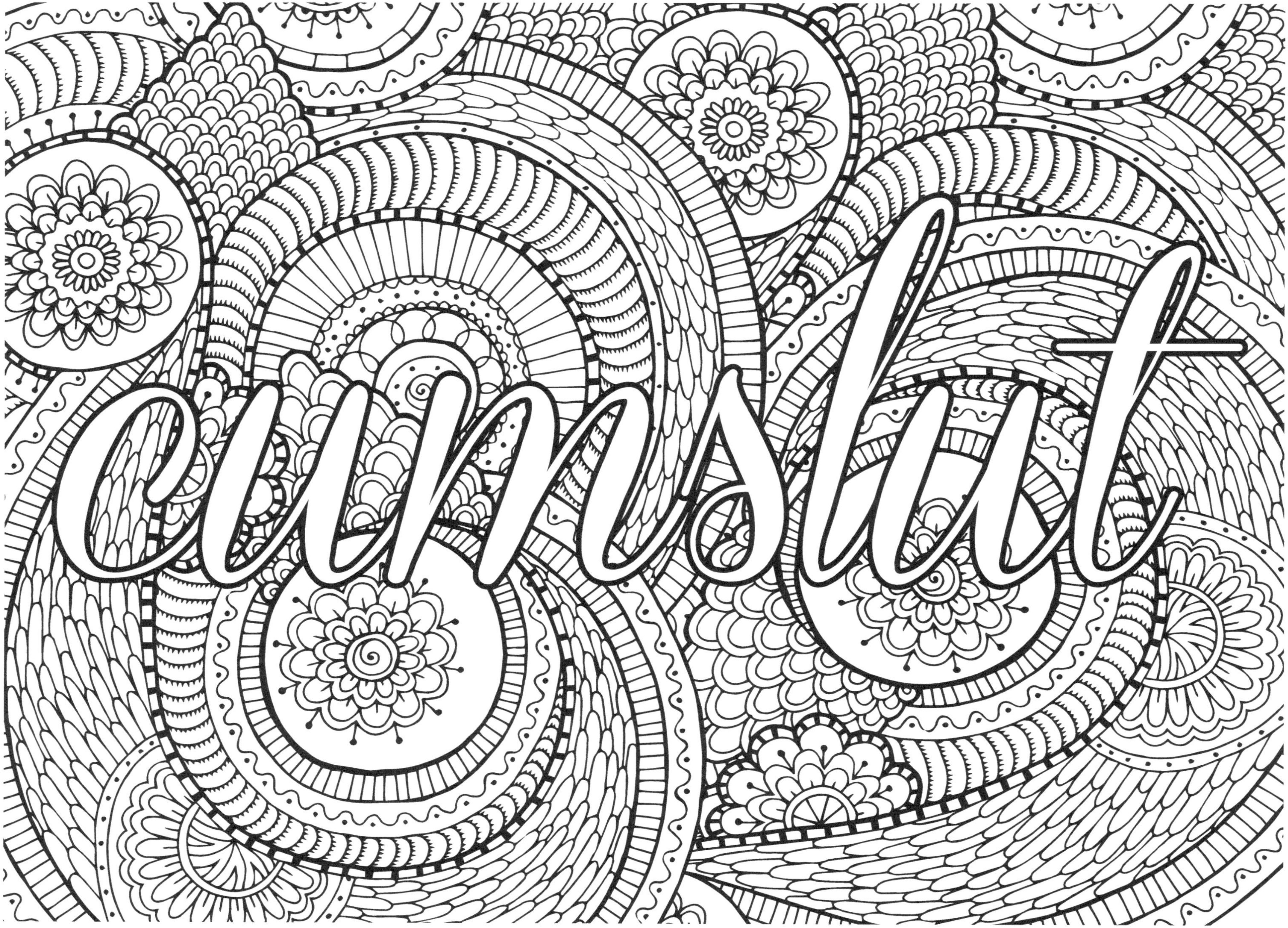
cumslut

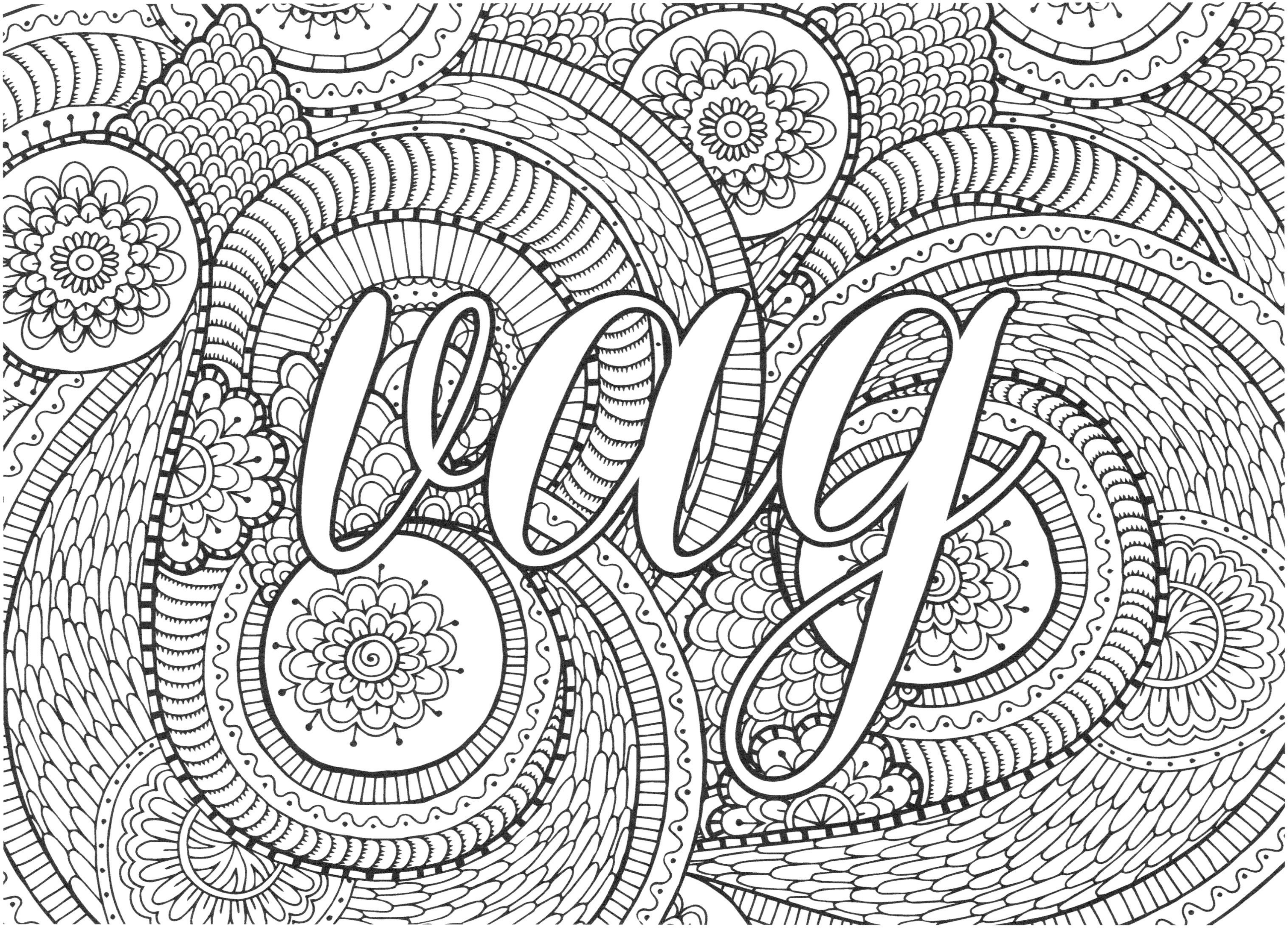

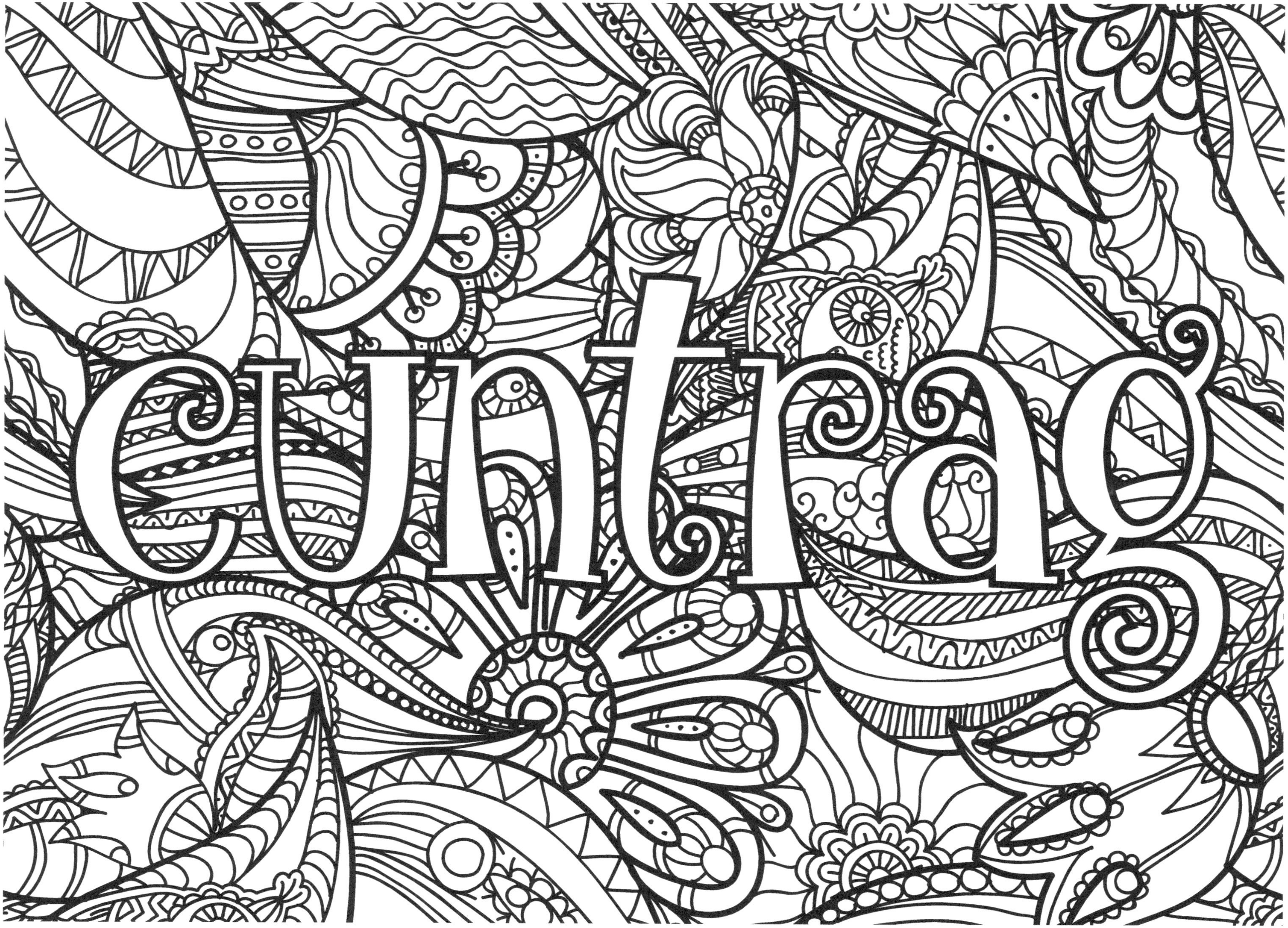
cuntrag

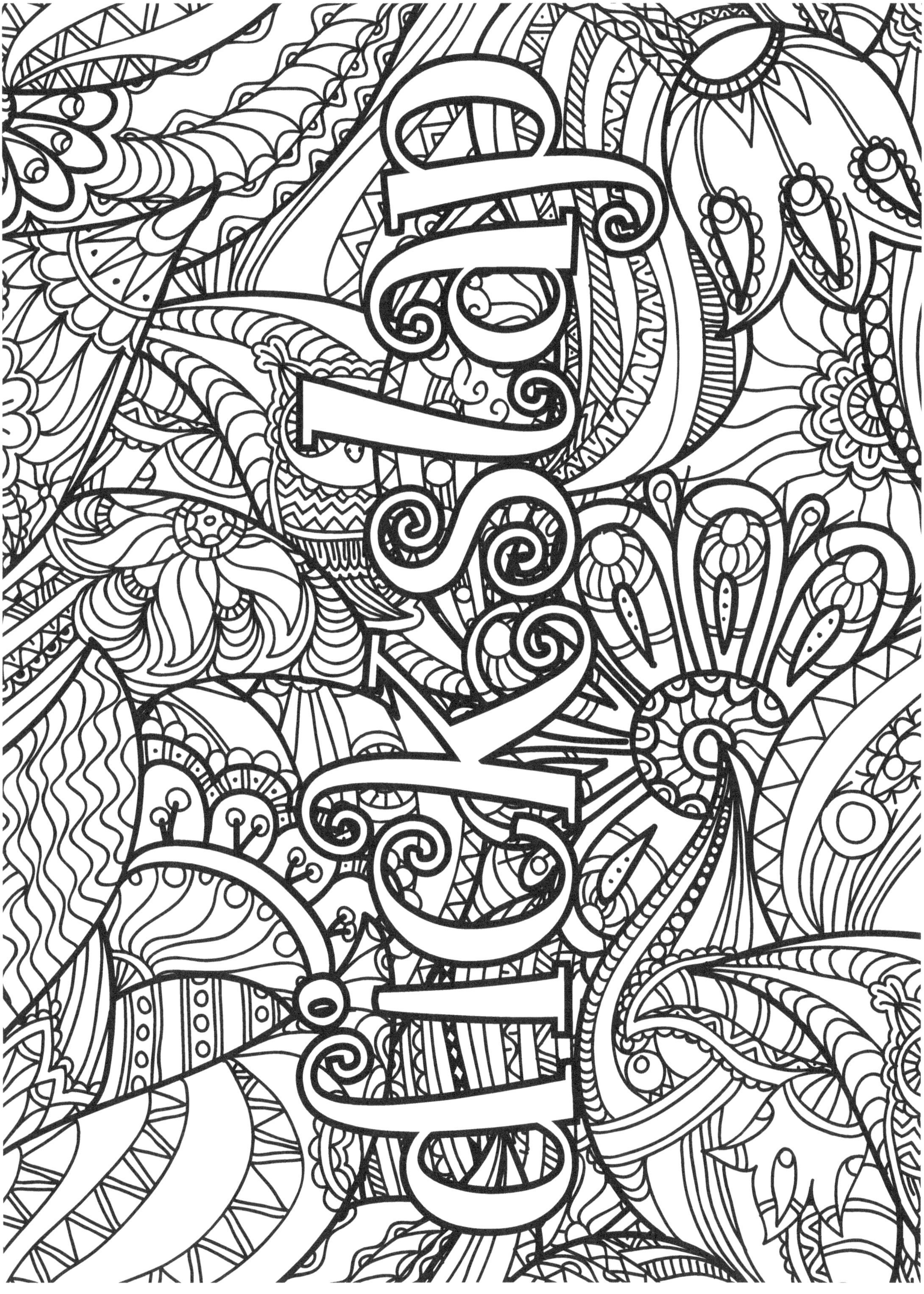
dickslap

This is a Bleed Through Page If You Are Using a Coloring Marker or Pen!
Find Other Great Titles By Us. Search on Your Favorite Book Retailer
Just search for the author name of Woodrow Guy .
He also Publishes Lite Erotica on Amazon Kindle

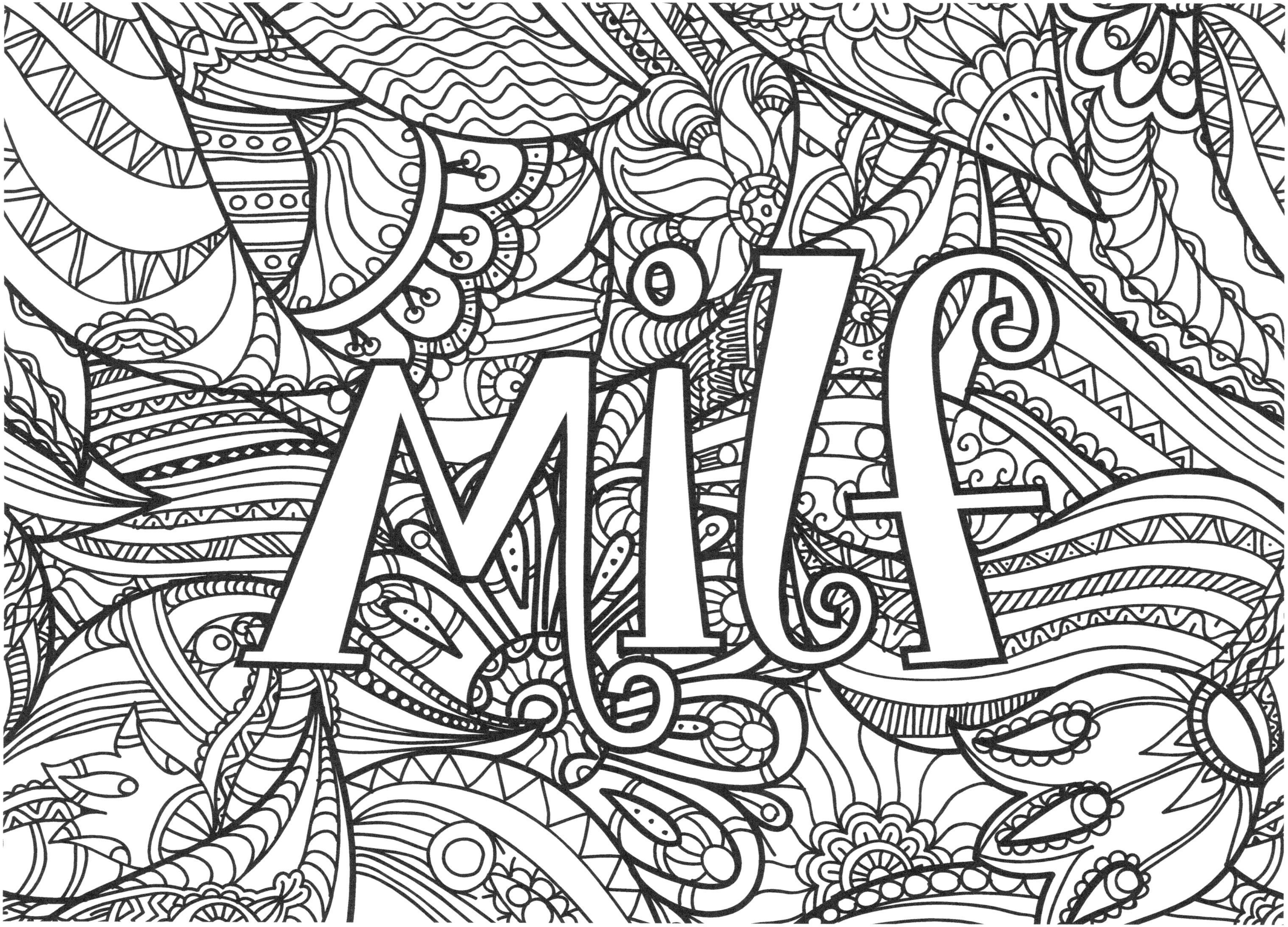
Milf

This is a Bleed Through Page If You Are Using a Coloring Marker or Pen!

Find Other Great Titles By Us. Search on Your Favorite Book Retailer

Just search for the author name of Woodrow Guy .

He also Publishes Lite Erotica on Amazon Kindle

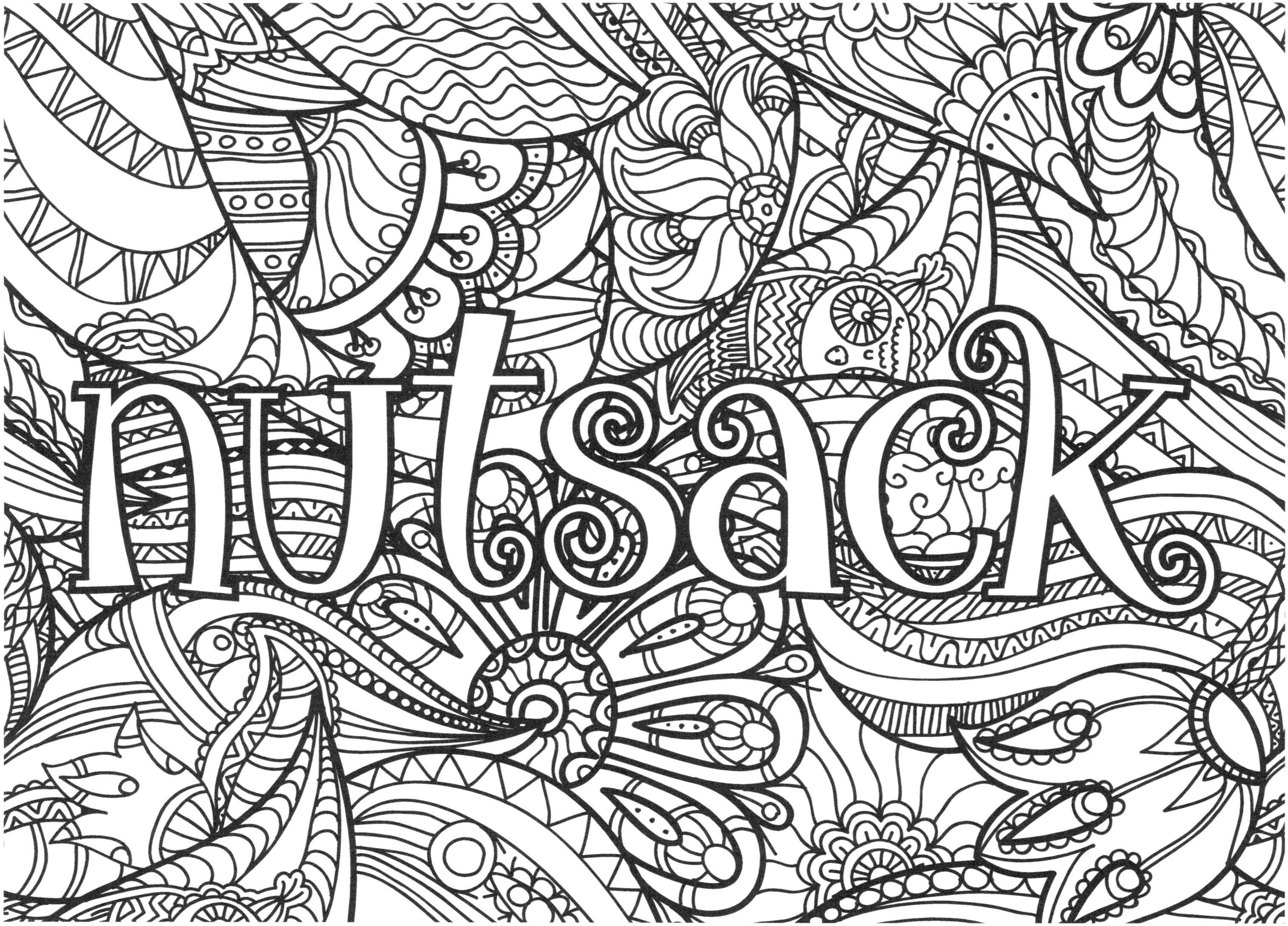
nutsack

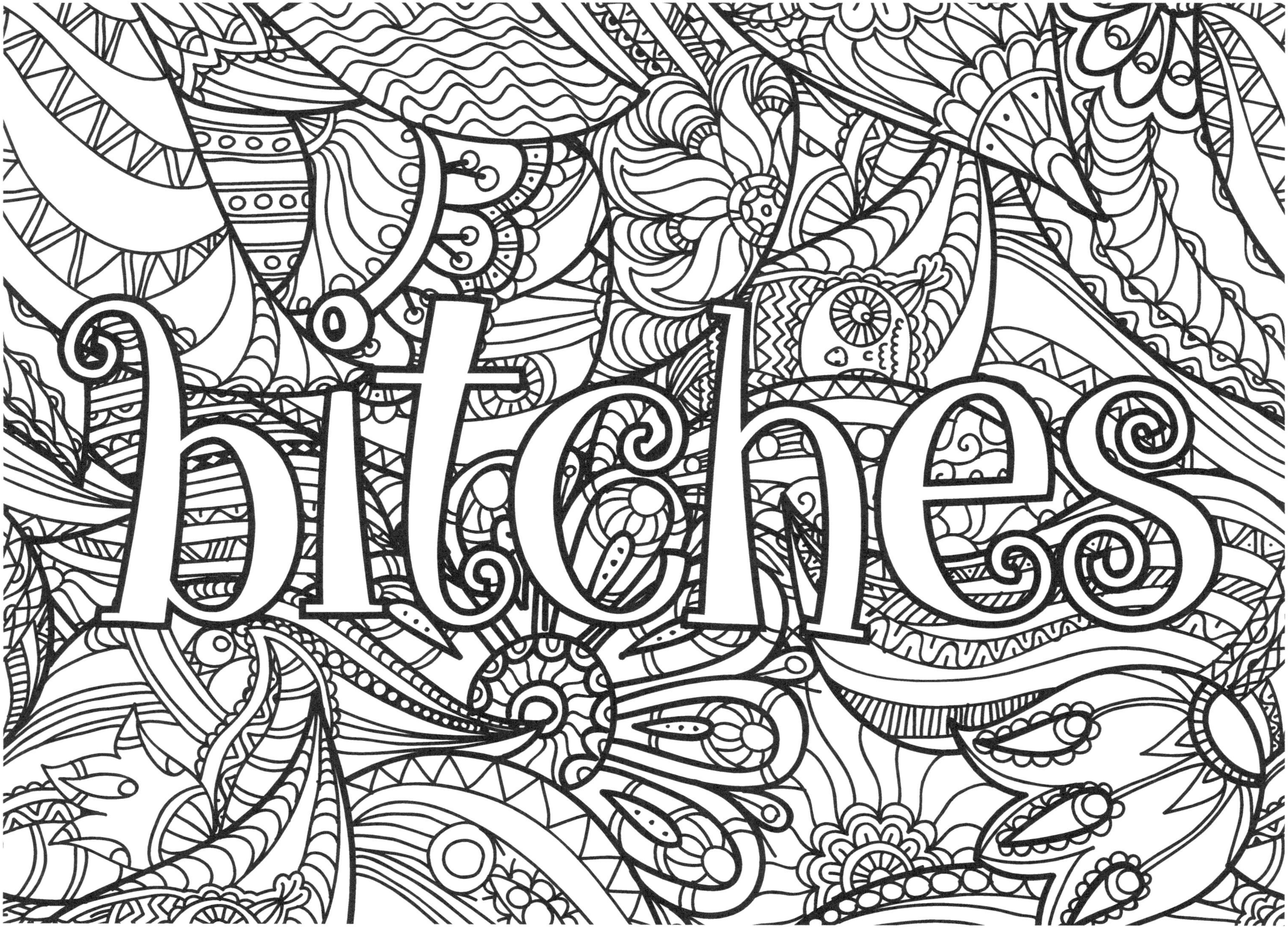
bitches

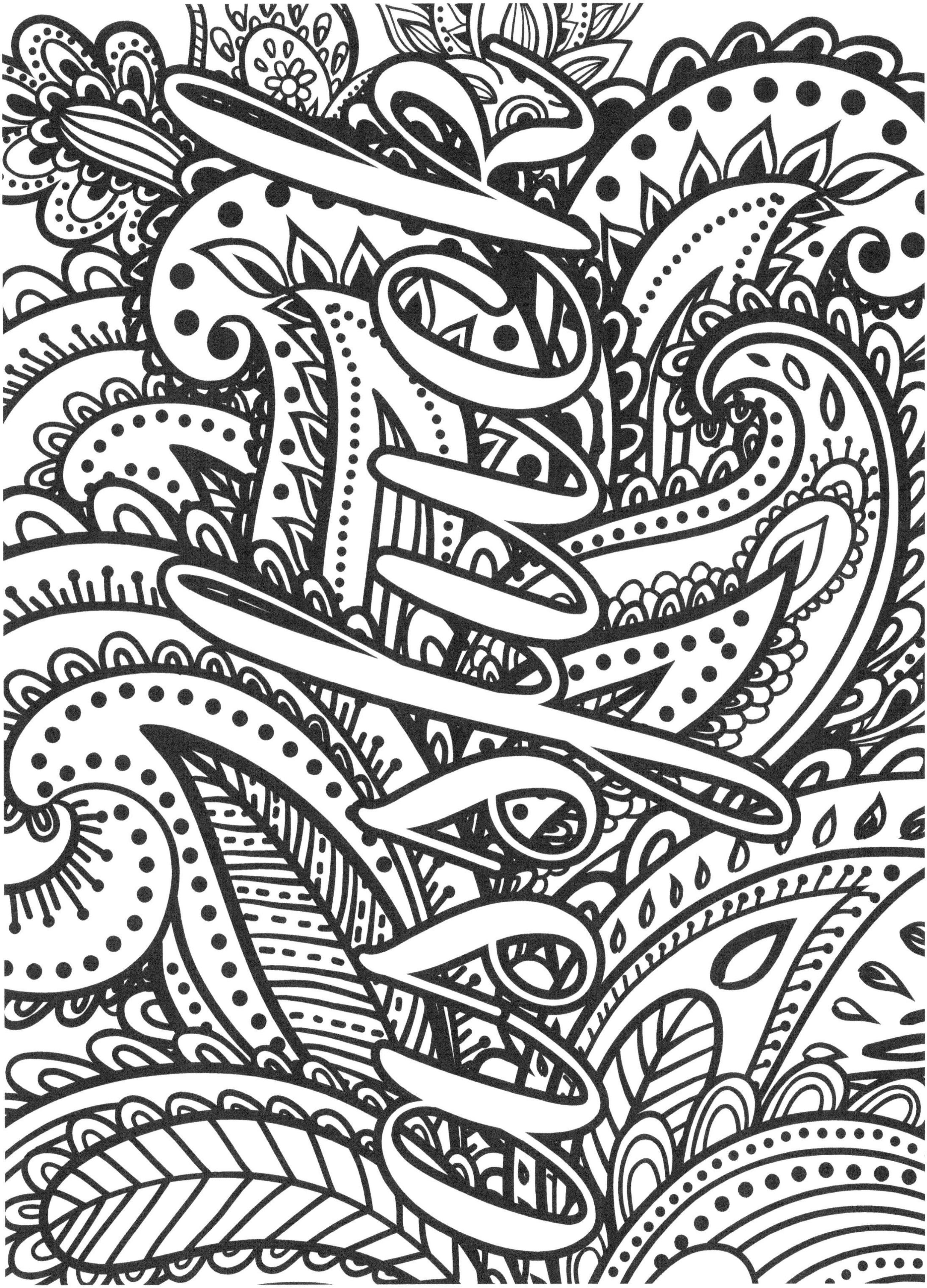

This is a Bleed Through Page If You Are Using a Coloring Marker or Pen!
Find Other Great Titles By Us. Search on Your Favorite Book Retailer
Just search for the author name of Woodrow Guy .
He also Publishes Lite Erotica on Amazon Kindle

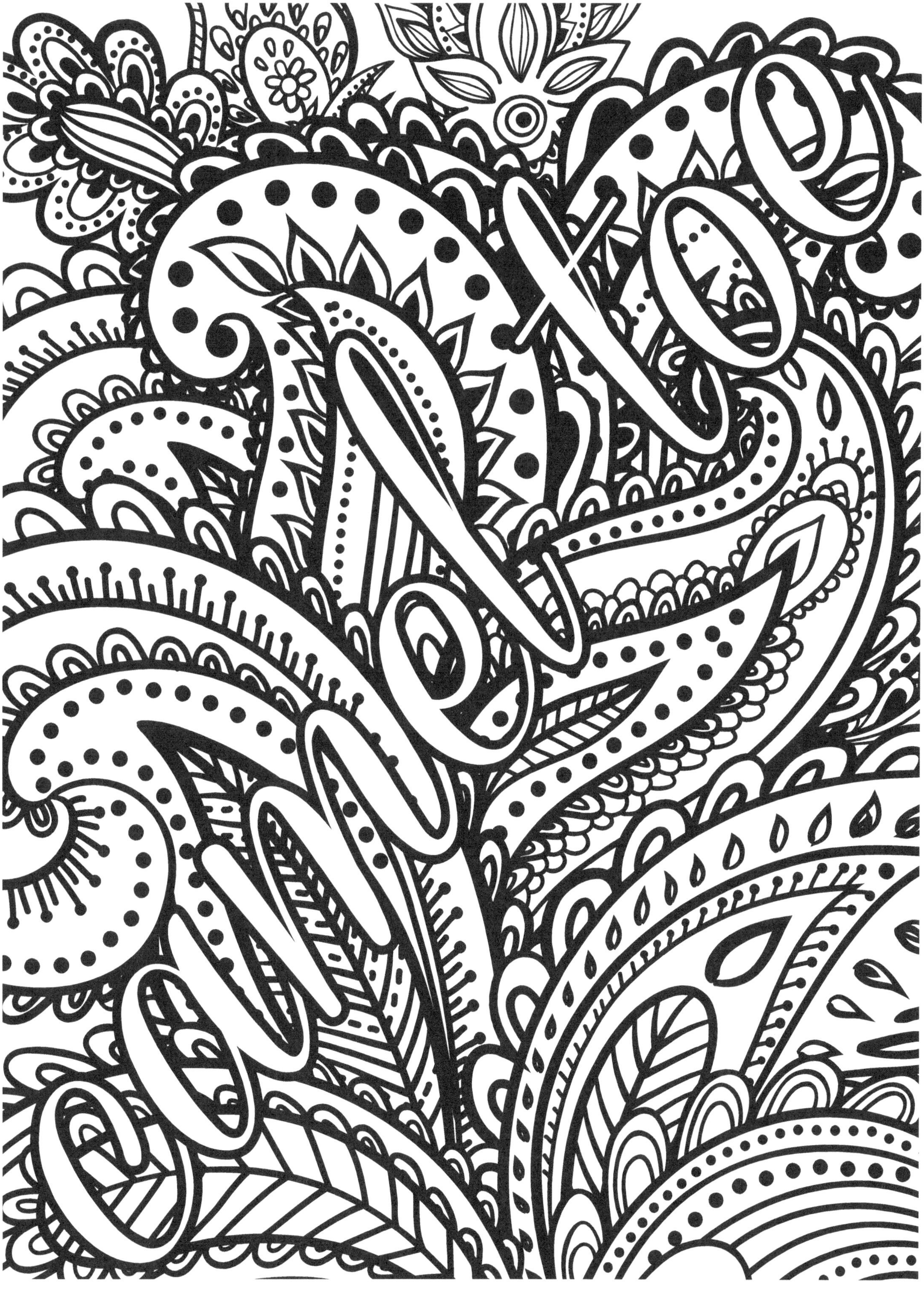

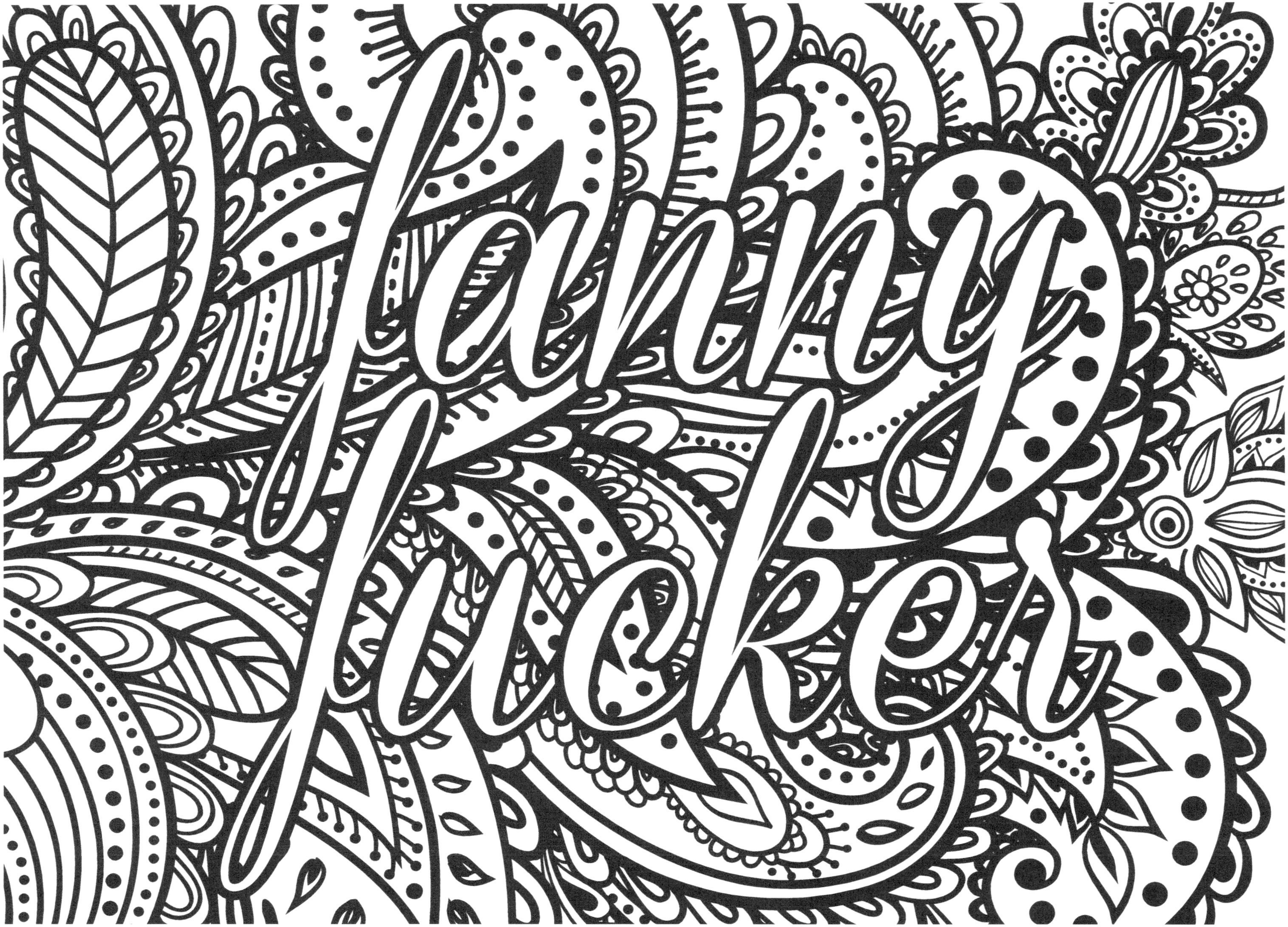
fanny
fucker

This is a Bleed Through Page If You Are Using a Coloring Marker or Pen!
Find Other Great Titles By Us. Search on Your Favorite Book Retailer
Just search for the author name of Woodrow Guy .
He also Publishes Lite Erotica on Amazon Kindle

www.ingramcontent.com/pod-product-compliance
Lightning Source LLC
Chambersburg PA
CBHW080546190526
45169CB00007B/2659
9781532881077